Awakening Leadership

In a time defined by complexity, disruption, and rapid innovation, *Awakening Leadership: The Journey to Conscious Influence* offers a transformative roadmap for leaders ready to rise with clarity, courage, and conscience. Merging timeless leadership principles with modern insights in emotional intelligence, mindfulness, ethical decision-making, and AI ethics, this book redefines how leaders influence, inspire, and impact the world around them.

Across fifteen compelling chapters, Dr. Mark Bojeun presents an integrated framework for conscious leadership—one that harmonizes performance with purpose and results with relationships. Readers will explore how to cultivate self-awareness, lead with authenticity, and build the emotional resilience necessary to thrive in uncertain environments. They will discover how to foster inclusive, values-driven cultures that ignite innovation, while learning to communicate with empathy, intentionality, and strategic presence. The book also provides guidance for navigating ambiguity, driving transformation, and leading with clarity in an increasingly AI-augmented world—all while aligning personal development with meaningful organizational impact.

Whether you are a senior executive refining your leadership presence, an emerging leader seeking deeper influence, or an educator preparing the next generation of changemakers, *Awakening Leadership: The Journey to Conscious Influence* delivers the mindset, structure, and tools to lead consciously and create a legacy built on trust, relevance, and purpose.

Lead with awareness. Influence with integrity. Transform with intention.

Dr. Mark Bojeun is a visionary technology executive, educator, and leadership strategist with more than 25 years of experience guiding enterprise transformation across government, higher education, and private industry. He is a recognized authority in AI integration, digital innovation, and building high-performing teams—leading initiatives that have redefined cloud strategy, cybersecurity, and organizational agility.

Holding a PhD in Organizational Behavior and an MBA, Dr. Bojeun also holds advanced certifications from the Project Management Institute, including PgMP, PMP, ACP, and RMP. As a global instructor, executive mentor, and architect of leadership education programs, he has trained thousands of leaders to navigate uncertainty, inspire trust, and create sustainable impact through conscious leadership.

Awakening Leadership
The Journey to Conscious Influence

Mark Bojeun, PhD

CRC Press
Taylor & Francis Group
Boca Raton London New York

CRC Press is an imprint of the
Taylor & Francis Group, an **informa** business

Designed cover image: Web Large Image (Public)

First edition published 2026
2385 NW Executive Center Drive, Suite 320, Boca Raton FL 33431

and by CRC Press
4 Park Square, Milton Park, Abingdon, Oxon, OX14 4RN

CRC Press is an imprint of Taylor & Francis Group, LLC

© 2026 Mark Bojeun

ISBN: 978-1-032-77551-7 (hbk)
ISBN: 978-1-032-78613-1 (pbk)
ISBN: 978-1-003-48870-5 (ebk)

DOI: 10.1201/9781003488705

Typeset in Minion
by codeMantra

Brené Brown

"To be a conscious leader, you must cultivate courage,

vulnerability, and empathy. Leadership is not about titles

or power, it's about the willingness to step up."

Contents

Preface

Awakening Leadership: The Journey to Conscious Influence is a seminal work that aims to redefine the landscape of leadership in today's complex and rapidly changing world. This book serves as a comprehensive guide, blending time-honored leadership principles with contemporary insights to offer a transformative pathway to becoming a more effective, authentic, and impactful leader. It is meticulously crafted to provide not just theoretical understanding but also practical tools and actionable strategies that can be applied in real-world leadership scenarios. This book covers a wide array of topics, from the importance of self-awareness and emotional intelligence to the transformative power of authenticity and vulnerability in leadership.

This book is structured to take the reader on a journey of self-discovery and growth. It starts with laying the foundational principles of conscious leadership, exploring its historical evolution and its critical importance in the modern world. Subsequent chapters delve into the core attributes that make up a conscious leader, such as self-awareness, emotional regulation, and ethical decision-making. Each chapter is enriched with case studies, self-assessment tools, and practical exercises to help readers internalize the concepts and apply them in their leadership roles.

The audience for this book is broad and diverse, encompassing current leaders, aspiring leaders, HR professionals, organizational consultants, and even educators in the field of leadership and management. Whether you are a seasoned executive looking to refine your leadership approach or an emerging leader aiming to develop a strong foundation, this book offers invaluable insights and guidance. It serves as a roadmap for those who are not just looking to improve their leadership skills but are also keen on fostering a culture of openness, innovation, and trust within their organizations.

What sets *Awakening Leadership* apart is its focus on the inner dimensions of leadership. While many leadership books offer strategies for external success—such as team management, strategic planning, and conflict resolution—this book emphasizes the inner work that is crucial for sustainable, effective leadership. It argues that true leadership influence stems from inner authenticity and conscious awareness, qualities that not only enhance personal effectiveness but also have the power to transform organizational culture.

Awakening Leadership: The Journey to Conscious Influence is more than just a book; it's a catalyst for change. It challenges the reader to rethink traditional notions of leadership, urging them to embrace a more conscious, authentic approach. With its blend of theoretical depth and practical applicability, it offers a holistic framework for leadership that is not just effective but also ethical and sustainable. It's a must-read for anyone committed to leading with integrity, empathy, and vision.

1

The Foundations of Conscious Leadership

HISTORICAL PERSPECTIVES ON LEADERSHIP

The landscape of leadership has been in a state of perpetual evolution, mirroring the complexities and demands of the societies it serves. From autocratic rulers in ancient civilizations to the industrial magnates of the 19th century, and now to the collaborative and emotionally intelligent leaders of today, the concept of what makes a good leader has shifted dramatically. This evolution reflects not just changes in our understanding of power dynamics, but also deeper shifts in our understanding of human psychology, social interaction, and even spiritual well-being.

The concept of leadership has been a topic of investigation and discussion for centuries. In ancient times, leaders were often born into their roles, and leadership was primarily a function of lineage and physical power. As societies progressed, our comprehension of what constitutes a good leader also evolved. The Great Man theory of the 19th century, which proposed that leaders are born, not made, yielded to the Trait theory, which aimed to identify the specific attributes that constitute a good leader. Over time, more sophisticated theories emerged, such as Transformational Leadership, which concentrates on the relationships between leaders and followers, and Servant Leadership, which inverts the traditional hierarchy to prioritize the needs of the team over those of the leader. Conscious Leadership can be perceived as an evolution of these theories, incorporating elements of emotional intelligence, ethical decision-making, and a focus on long-term sustainability (Figure 1.1).

DOI: 10.1201/9781003488705-1

Socratic
Philosophy (400
BC): "Know
Thyself"

Goleman's
Emotional
Intelligence:
Emotional
Intelligence
Framework

Maslow's
Hierarchy
(1943): Self-
actualization at
the pinnacle

Modern
Practices
(2000s):
Mindfulness and
reflective
leadership

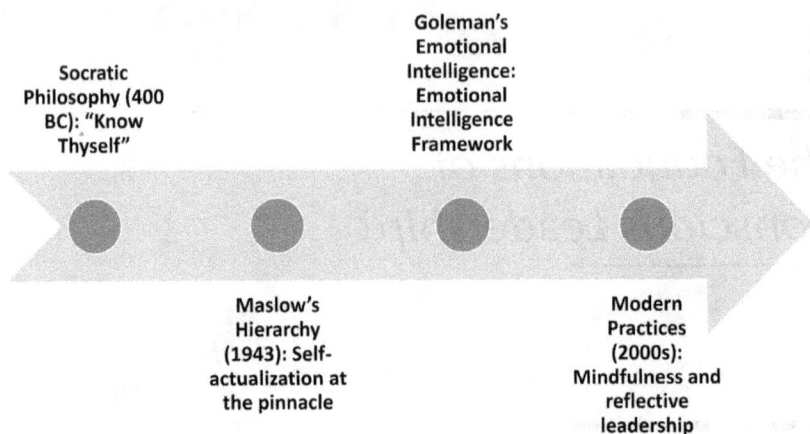

FIGURE 1.1
The Evolution of Self-awareness in Leadership.

DEFINING CONSCIOUS LEADERSHIP

Conscious Leadership is a phrase that has garnered significant attention in recent years, but what does it truly signify? At its heart, Conscious Leadership is about cognizance. It's about being aware not only of your own actions, thoughts, and emotions but also of the individuals around you and the larger systems in which you function. It's leadership that surpasses the transactional components of the role to embrace a more comprehensive, ethical, and empathetic approach.

In today's fast-paced, interconnected world, the relevance of Conscious Leadership has never been more pronounced. The challenges we face—be it climate change, social inequality, or the rapid pace of technological advancement—require leaders who are not just skilled in strategy and execution but are also aware of the broader impact of their decisions. Conscious Leadership fills this gap by emphasizing not just the 'what' and the 'how,' but also the 'why.' It calls for a holistic approach that combines traditional leadership skills with emotional intelligence, ethical decision-making, and a focus on long-term sustainability.

The concept of Conscious Leadership has evolved over time, influenced by various disciplines, philosophies, and leadership theories. While it's difficult to pinpoint a single origin, the term gained prominence in the early 21st century, particularly with the rise of conscious capitalism, a term popularized by John Mackey, the co-founder of Whole Foods, and Raj Sisodia, a thought leader in the field. Their work emphasized the importance of purpose-driven, ethical business practices that benefit all stakeholders, not just shareholders. Conscious Leadership serves as the human element in the conscious capitalism equation, focusing on the role leaders play in creating a conscious business culture.

However, the roots of Conscious Leadership can be traced back to much older philosophies and spiritual traditions. Concepts like mindfulness, self-awareness, and Servant Leadership have ancient origins, found in Eastern philosophies like Buddhism and Taoism as well as in religious teachings like those of Jesus Christ, who exemplified Servant Leadership.

In the latter half of the 20th century, the human potential movement, which emphasized self-actualization and human capacity, also influenced the development of Conscious Leadership. Leaders in psychology like Carl Rogers and Abraham Maslow laid the groundwork by exploring the potential of human consciousness and the hierarchy of needs, respectively. Their work indirectly contributed to the understanding that leadership could be a path of personal growth and self-realization, not just a means to an end.

The field of organizational development also played a role, particularly the work around emotional intelligence. Daniel Goleman's seminal work in the 1990s brought emotional intelligence to the forefront of leadership development. This dovetailed nicely with the principles of Conscious Leadership, which also emphasizes self-awareness, self-regulation, and empathy.

In recent years, the concept has gained traction with the rise of social entrepreneurship, corporate social responsibility, and a greater focus on workplace well-being. The challenges of the 21st century—such as climate change, social inequality, and the mental health crisis—have made it increasingly clear that a new kind of leadership is needed, one that is not only effective but also ethical, compassionate, and aware.

Today, Conscious Leadership is taught in business schools and leadership development programs, and it's practiced in organizations around the world. It has been the subject of numerous books, articles, and academic studies that explore its principles, its effectiveness, and its impact on organizational culture and performance.

In essence, Conscious Leadership is a synthesis of age-old wisdom and modern psychology, business strategy, and organizational behavior. It represents a shift from a mechanistic, transactional view of leadership to a more holistic, relational, and purpose-driven paradigm, one that holds the promise of not just greater financial success but also greater well-being for individuals and society at large.

With these considerations in mind, this book aims to be a comprehensive guide to Conscious Leadership, a leadership style that is both timely and timeless. It is designed to offer a blend of theoretical understanding, practical tools, and real-world examples to help you navigate the complex yet rewarding landscape of Conscious Leadership.

The first chapter serves as an introduction to the concept, tracing the historical evolution of leadership theories and pinpointing where Conscious Leadership fits within this rich tapestry. It aims to define Conscious Leadership and outline the principles that underpin it, setting the stage for the deeper explorations that follow.

Chapter 2 zeroes in on self-awareness, often considered the cornerstone of Conscious Leadership. This chapter not only underscores the importance of being aware of one's own thoughts, emotions, and actions but also provides practical tools for cultivating this crucial skill.

As we move to Chapter 3, the focus shifts to authenticity and vulnerability, two qualities that are often overlooked in traditional leadership models. Here, we explore how showing your true self and embracing your vulnerabilities can actually be a source of strength, fostering trust and deeper connections with your team.

Mindfulness, the practice of being fully present, is the subject of Chapter 4. This chapter offers practical exercises to help you integrate mindfulness into your leadership style, thereby improving decision-making and reducing stress.

Chapter 5 delves into the roles of empathy and compassion in leadership. It explores how understanding and sharing the feelings of others can lead to more effective and humane leadership, offering case studies that bring these concepts to life.

The art of conscious communication is dissected in Chapter 6. This chapter provides actionable strategies for communicating in a mindful and empathetic manner, skills that are particularly useful in conflict resolution and during difficult conversations.

Chapter 7 examines the relationship between Servant Leadership and Conscious Leadership, highlighting both their similarities and differences. Through real-world examples, this chapter shows how the principles of Conscious Leadership can enhance and deepen the practice of Servant Leadership.

Chapter 8 focuses on the ripple effect that Conscious Leadership can have on organizational culture. It offers strategies for aligning your organization's values with its actions and provides case studies of companies that have successfully created cultures of consciousness.

The challenges that come with practicing Conscious Leadership are the focus of Chapter 9. This chapter aims to prepare you for the hurdles you may encounter, offering strategies for overcoming resistance and skepticism.

Chapter 10 discusses how to measure and evaluate the effectiveness of your Conscious Leadership practices. It emphasizes the importance of feedback and continuous improvement, providing guidelines for developing meaningful metrics.

Chapter 11 brings the theories and practices discussed in the previous chapters into the real world. Through interviews with practicing conscious leaders, this chapter offers a more practical perspective, providing tips and lessons learned from those who have successfully integrated Conscious Leadership into their professional lives.

Chapter 12 looks to the future, exploring how the principles of Conscious Leadership can be spread more broadly. It outlines a vision for a more conscious future, emphasizing the far-reaching impact that even one conscious leader can have on an organization and, by extension, society.

Chapter 13 explores how Conscious Leadership principles apply during times of organizational change and uncertainty. It provides tools and strategies to maintain clarity, resilience, and adaptability when leading through ambiguity, and offers case studies that highlight effective, conscious approaches to managing transition.

Chapter 14 examines the intersection of technology and leadership, discussing both the potential and limitations of AI and digital tools in leadership contexts. It emphasizes ethical considerations, digital empathy, and the role of conscious leaders in shaping tech-driven cultures responsibly and sustainably.

Chapter 15 addresses the critical responsibility leaders have toward social and environmental sustainability. It introduces the concept of the triple bottom line—people, planet, and profit—and illustrates how Conscious Leadership can drive meaningful, purpose-aligned business practices with far-reaching impact.

The goal of this book is to serve as a comprehensive guide to Conscious Leadership, offering a balanced blend of theory, practical tools, and real-world insights. It is designed to equip both current and aspiring leaders with the knowledge and skills they need to lead in a more conscious, ethical, and effective manner.

CORE PRINCIPLES OF CONSCIOUS LEADERSHIP

Management is doing things right; leadership is doing the right things.
– Peter Drucker

This quote encapsulates the essence of Conscious Leadership, which goes beyond mere efficiency and effectiveness to consider the ethical and emotional dimensions of leadership. It serves as a reminder that Conscious Leadership is not just about achieving goals but about the manner and the principles that guide how those goals are achieved.

There are four principles that are used to drive Conscious Leadership

- Self-awareness
- Authenticity
- Mindfulness
- Growth and learning

First and foremost is self-awareness. A conscious leader is deeply attuned to their own inner landscape and is able to navigate their emotions, thoughts, and actions with a sense of purpose and integrity. This self-awareness extends outward to an awareness of others, fostering empathy and compassionate action (Figure 1.2).

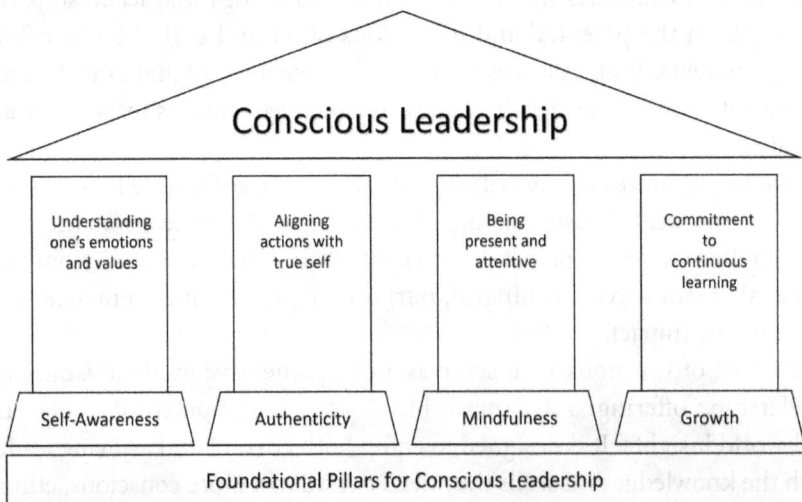

Conscious Leadership

Understanding one's emotions and values	Aligning actions with true self	Being present and attentive	Commitment to continuous learning
Self-Awareness	Authenticity	Mindfulness	Growth

Foundational Pillars for Conscious Leadership

FIGURE 1.2
The Four Pillars of Self-awareness.

Conscious leaders are true to themselves and their values, and they are not afraid to show vulnerability. This authenticity creates a culture of trust and openness, where team members feel safe expressing their own ideas and concerns.

Mindfulness involves being fully present in the moment, which allows for more thoughtful decision-making and a greater ability to manage stress. Mindfulness practices, such as meditation or mindful breathing, can be powerful tools for developing this skill.

Finally, a commitment to continuous growth and learning is essential. The landscape of business and leadership is ever-changing, and a conscious leader is always looking for ways to adapt and improve, both on a personal level and in terms of their leadership practice.

Conscious Leadership is not just a buzzword; it's a nuanced approach to leadership that requires a deep understanding of oneself and the world. It builds on the theories of leadership that have come before it, incorporating the best elements of each while adding a layer of emotional and ethical intelligence. As we move forward into an increasingly complex and interconnected world, the principles of Conscious Leadership offer a roadmap for leading with integrity, compassion, and a deep sense of purpose.

Conscious Leadership also places a strong emphasis on the collective well-being of the organization and its stakeholders. This is a departure from more traditional, hierarchical models of leadership that often prioritize profits or short-term gains over the welfare of employees, customers, or the community. A conscious leader recognizes that an organization is a system of interconnected parts, and that the well-being of one affects the well-being of all. This systemic thinking extends beyond the walls of the organization to include societal and environmental impacts, aligning with the broader goals of sustainability and social responsibility.

THE CONSCIOUS LEADER'S MINDSET

One principle that is integral to Conscious Leadership is open and effective communication. This goes beyond merely transmitting information. Conscious leaders engage in dialogue rather than monologue. They listen actively, ask questions, and create a space where team members feel heard and valued. This fosters a culture of inclusion and collaboration, where diverse perspectives are not just tolerated but actively sought out and celebrated.

They leverage Emotional Intelligence (EQ) and Mindfulness to be present in the conversation and to "hear" the unspoken from body language to tone and word choices. The conscious leader leaves other issues and individuals behind and is 100% involved and present in the current communication reducing bias, perception, and agendas.

Moreover, conscious leaders are adept at conflict resolution and are not afraid to tackle difficult conversations head-on. They approach conflicts as opportunities for growth and learning, rather than as threats. This involves a high degree of emotional intelligence, as the leader must be able to manage their own emotions while also navigating the emotional landscape of their team.

Ethical decision-making is also a hallmark of Conscious Leadership. This involves a commitment to doing what's right, even when it's not easy or popular. Ethical considerations are integrated into all aspects of decision-making, from strategy formulation to daily operations. This also means taking responsibility for one's actions and consequences, both intended and unintended.

This leadership model is not static but a dynamic process of ongoing growth and development. It involves a commitment to personal and professional development, a willingness to question one's assumptions and beliefs, and the humility to admit when one is wrong. Continuous feedback loops, both formal and informal, are essential for this kind of growth. These can be regular performance reviews, 360-degree feedback, or an open-door policy where team members feel comfortable sharing their thoughts and concerns.

It is a multifaceted approach that builds upon the best elements of previous leadership theories while incorporating a deeper layer of awareness, ethics, and emotional intelligence. Its principles are theoretical constructs and actionable guidelines that can be integrated into daily leadership practice. As we navigate the complexities of the modern world, with its myriad challenges and opportunities, Conscious Leadership offers an effective, meaningful, and fulfilling way to lead. It provides a framework for leadership that is not just about achieving goals but about elevating the entire human experience, both within the organization and in the broader world.

Ethical decision-making is a cornerstone of Conscious Leadership, serving as the moral compass that guides actions and choices. Unlike traditional leadership models, where ethics might be a secondary consideration to profitability or efficiency, ethical considerations are integrated into decision-making processes in Conscious Leadership. This is not merely a matter of compliance with laws and regulations, but a deeper commitment to doing what is right, fair, and just for all stakeholders involved.

A conscious leader faces a complex landscape of ethical dilemmas, often having to navigate conflicting demands and priorities. For instance, consider a situation where maximizing shareholder value conflicts with environmental sustainability goals. A traditional leader might prioritize the former at the expense of the latter, but a conscious leader would seek a more balanced approach. They might look for innovative solutions that both drive profitability and are environmentally sustainable, recognizing that long-term success requires a harmonious relationship with the community and the planet.

When faced with conflicting demands, a conscious leader employs a nuanced, multi-step approach to decision-making. First, they would engage in self-reflection to understand their own biases and preconceptions that could influence the decision. This is where the principle of self-awareness comes into play. By being aware of their own inner landscape, conscious leaders are better equipped to make impartial decisions.

Next, they would gather as much information as possible, consulting not just with senior management but also with team members, and even external stakeholders when appropriate. This aligns with the principle of open communication and inclusion, valuing diverse perspectives and expertise.

Once all the information is gathered, the leader would weigh the various options, considering both short-term and long-term consequences for all stakeholders involved. This is where the principle of systemic thinking becomes crucial. A conscious leader understands that every decision has a ripple effect, impacting not just the immediate situation but also the broader system in which the organization operates. After careful consideration, the leader would decide and take responsibility for it, prepared to face any positive or negative consequences. This aligns with the principle of authenticity and vulnerability, as the leader is not afraid to make tough decisions and stand by them.

As a last step, the leader would engage in a feedback loop, evaluating the outcomes of the decision and making adjustments as necessary. This reflects the principle of continuous growth and learning, recognizing that ethical decision-making is not a one-time event but an ongoing process.

Ethical decision-making in Conscious Leadership is a complex, multilayered process that involves a deep understanding of oneself, a commitment to open communication and inclusion, a systemic approach to problem-solving, and a willingness to take responsibility for one's actions. By integrating these principles into their decision-making processes, conscious leaders are better equipped to navigate the ethical complexities of the modern world, leading in an effective and morally sound way.

Intentional leadership emerges as a closely intertwined concept in the realm of Conscious Leadership. Within the framework of Conscious Leadership, intentional leadership often takes center stage as a fundamental component, shaping how leaders approach their roles and responsibilities.

Conscious Leadership, at its core, is a holistic philosophy that places a premium on self-awareness, mindfulness, and purpose-driven decision-making. It calls upon leaders to be fully present in each moment, to delve deep into an understanding of their values and motivations, and to lead with an unwavering commitment to authenticity and empathy. It's a leadership style that transcends the mundane and delves into the profound.

Intentionality stands as a pivotal pillar within the structure of Conscious Leadership. Being intentional means far more than merely going through the motions; it entails setting clear and meaningful intentions for every action, decision, and interaction. It's the art of aligning one's deeds with their core values and the grand vision they hold for themselves and their organizations.

Intentional and Conscious Leadership find common ground in their unwavering commitment to values alignment. Leaders who embrace intentional leadership carefully craft their choices to mirror their values, forging a path of consistency and authenticity in their leadership journey. This synergy of values alignment propels leaders toward a profound resonance with their purpose.

Mindful decision-making, a hallmark of Conscious Leadership, fits seamlessly into the intentional leadership paradigm. Leaders who practice intentionality approach every decision with meticulous thoughtfulness, pausing to reflect on the potential ripples their choices might create. These leaders navigate the complexities of leadership with a clear purpose and an acute awareness of the long-term ramifications of their actions.

Vision and purpose radiate from conscious leaders, driven by an unwavering sense of mission. Intentional leadership complements this by urging leaders to set explicit intentions and work diligently toward achieving their objectives. This harmonious fusion of purpose and intentionality ignites a sense of direction that guides their every step.

The tapestry of authenticity and empathy is intricately woven into both intentional and Conscious Leadership. Leaders who embrace these principles seek to forge profound connections with others, striving to understand and relate on a deeper level. They cultivate trust and collaboration within their teams, nurturing environments where individuals can thrive.

Personal growth and development are constant companions on the journey of Conscious Leadership. This approach encourages leaders to view self-awareness as an ongoing odyssey. Intentional leadership dovetails with this notion, promoting introspection and continual evolution to ensure that leaders align with their intentions.

Ultimately, intentional leadership emerges as a formidable tool wielded by conscious leaders to magnify their positive impact. By setting clear intentions and forging actions in harmony with their values, they cultivate an ecosystem in which individuals and organizations flourish. It is in this unity of intentionality and consciousness that authentic, empathetic, and purpose-driven leaders emerge, poised to usher their teams and organizations toward greater heights.

THE "DARK" SIDE

An unconscious leader is often reactive rather than proactive, driven by ego rather than by a desire to serve, and focused on short-term gains rather than long-term sustainability. Such leaders may be unaware of their own biases, emotions, and triggers, and this lack of self-awareness often extends to a lack of empathy and understanding of others. They may engage in what's known as "autopilot leadership," making decisions based on habit or convenience rather than thoughtful consideration.

Unconscious leaders often prioritize their own needs or the needs of a select few over the collective well-being of their team or organization. This can manifest in various ways, from taking credit for others' work to ignoring or even suppressing dissenting opinions.

Communication is often one-way, with little room for feedback or open dialogue. This creates a culture of fear and disengagement, where team members feel undervalued and unheard.

Now, one might argue that all poor leadership is damaging, so what makes unconscious leadership particularly pernicious? The answer lies in the gap between rhetoric and reality. An unconscious leader may be well-versed in the language of modern leadership theories, including Conscious Leadership, and may even preach these principles to their team. However, if these principles are not reflected in their actions, the disconnect can be incredibly demoralizing for team members. It's the difference between a leader who is simply ineffective and one who is perceived as hypocritical. The latter can be far more destructive because it erodes trust, not just in the leader but in the very principles they espouse.

This form of leadership can be particularly damaging in organizations that are going through change or facing significant challenges. In such contexts, the need for authentic, Conscious Leadership is heightened. An unconscious leader can exacerbate tensions, deepen divisions, and contribute to a toxic culture that hampers productivity and well-being.

Unconscious leadership is not merely the absence of Conscious Leadership but a set of behaviors and attitudes that can be actively harmful. It's characterized by a lack of self-awareness, a focus on short-term gains at the expense of long-term sustainability, and a failure to walk the talk when it comes to ethical and empathetic leadership. Understanding the traits of unconscious leadership can serve as a cautionary tale, highlighting the importance of striving for greater awareness and integrity in our own leadership practices.

The impact of unconscious leadership on team dynamics and organizational culture can be profound and far-reaching. Team members working under such a leader often experience a decline in morale, engagement, and productivity. The lack of authentic communication and openness can lead to an environment where employees feel they cannot speak their minds or offer constructive criticism. This stifling atmosphere can suppress creativity and innovation, as team members may become risk-averse, fearing repercussions for stepping out of line or challenging the status quo.

Moreover, the absence of ethical decision-making and a focus on short-term gains can create ethical dilemmas for team members. They may find themselves torn between following directives they disagree with and risking their job security. This ethical dissonance can lead to increased stress and job dissatisfaction, further eroding engagement and productivity.

The ripple effects of unconscious leadership can extend beyond the immediate team to impact the broader organizational culture. When leaders do not practice what they preach, cynicism can set in, leading employees to question the integrity of not just their leader but the organization as a whole. This erosion of trust can have serious implications, including increased turnover, reduced collaboration between departments, and even reputational damage that affects customer trust and shareholder value.

In a worst-case scenario, the negative impacts of unconscious leadership can become deeply ingrained in the organizational culture, creating a toxic work environment that is resistant to change. In such cultures, negative behaviors and attitudes are not just tolerated but normalized, making it extremely difficult to implement positive change. This can create a vicious cycle where poor leadership begets poor performance, which, in turn, reinforces poor leadership, and so on.

In contrast, Conscious Leadership fosters a culture of trust, openness, and mutual respect, where each team member feels valued and empowered. The positive impacts on team dynamics and organizational culture are manifold, from increased engagement and productivity to enhanced creativity and innovation. Moreover, organizations led by conscious leaders are better equipped to navigate the complexities and challenges of the modern business landscape, from ethical dilemmas to rapid technological change.

The impact of unconscious leadership on team dynamics and organizational culture can be devastating, leading to disengagement, ethical dissonance, and even a toxic work environment. Understanding these negative impacts underscores the importance of Conscious Leadership as a means of fostering a more positive, productive, and ethical organizational culture.

Conscious Leadership calls for a deep level of self-awareness, a quality that is often easier said than achieved. Two significant barriers to attaining this awareness are defensive mechanisms and emotional triggers. While they serve as our mind's way of coping with uncomfortable truths or situations, they can also be significant roadblocks on the path to becoming a conscious leader.

A large government-contracting firm had a leader named Alex. Alex was widely known for being a walking encyclopedia of management approaches and leadership theories. They could passionately discuss the latest management trends, recommend books on leadership, and even teach workshops on various management styles. Many considered Alex a true guru of leadership knowledge.

People admired Alex's intellect and were eager to learn from them. The team would often gather around Alex, seeking advice on different management approaches. Alex would eloquently explain the principles of Conscious Leadership, emphasizing the importance of self-awareness, empathy, and aligning actions with values. Their explanations were so compelling that everyone believed they embodied these principles.

However, as time passed, a stark contrast between Alex's words and actions became apparent. While they advocated for Conscious Leadership, their behavior didn't reflect it. In meetings, Alex often dominated discussions, rarely allowing others to voice their opinions. They would dismiss feedback and decisions made collectively, believing their ideas were superior.

Despite speaking about empathy, Alex failed to connect with team members on a personal level. They seemed distant and aloof, rarely showing genuine interest in the well-being of their colleagues. It became evident that

Alex's actions didn't align with their eloquent speeches on empathy and understanding.

One day, a significant challenge arose within the organization. The team faced a difficult decision that required empathy, collaboration, and a Conscious Leadership approach. It was a defining moment for Alex to practice what they preached. However, when the pressure was on, Alex reverted to an autocratic style of leadership, making unilateral decisions without considering others' perspectives.

This incident shook the team's trust in Alex. They realized that despite all the knowledge and eloquence, their leader's actions contradicted Conscious Leadership principles. The team began to question whether the words and theories that Alex preached were just empty rhetoric.

In the end, Alex's credibility as a leader was tarnished. The gap between their knowledge and their actions became too glaring to ignore. The team longed for a leader who not only spoke about Conscious Leadership but also embodied it in their daily actions.

This story serves as a reminder that leadership is not defined by what one knows or says but by how one consistently behaves and the values they uphold. It illustrates the importance of aligning words with actions and living the principles of Conscious Leadership for genuine and lasting impact.

Conscious Leadership outlines a model that is supportive, understanding, empathetic, and ethical in the day-to-day approach used to leading people. But understanding the opposite of Conscious Leadership—often termed "unconscious leadership"—can provide a stark contrast that illuminates the importance of leading consciously. Just as Conscious Leadership works to build a team actively and through an empathetic, respectful, inclusive approach, unconscious leadership is as adept at destroying the team effectiveness, eroding trust in the leader, and creating a culture of fear and disengagement.

DEFENSIVE MECHANISMS: THE MASKS WE WEAR

Defensive mechanisms like denial, projection, and rationalization are psychological strategies we unconsciously employ to protect our self-esteem or ego. For example, a leader who is unable to meet project deadlines might rationalize the delays by blaming external factors, thereby absolving themselves of any responsibility. While such mechanisms can offer short-term emotional relief, they hinder genuine self-awareness by obscuring the truth about ourselves and our actions.

In the realm of Conscious Leadership, these defensive mechanisms can be particularly detrimental. They not only prevent us from seeing ourselves clearly but can also distort our perception of others and the situations we encounter. This lack of clarity can lead to poor decision-making, strained relationships, and ultimately, a leadership style that is neither authentic nor effective.

EMOTIONAL TRIGGERS: THE LANDMINES IN OUR PSYCHE

Emotional triggers are specific events, situations, or behaviors that evoke strong emotional reactions. These triggers can cloud our judgment and make objective self-assessment difficult. When triggered, people are more likely to act on impulse, making decisions that align with their emotional state rather than their true values or objectives. For instance, a leader who is triggered by perceived challenges to their authority might react defensively or aggressively, thereby escalating conflicts instead of resolving them.

The impact of emotional triggers extends beyond the individual leader. A triggered leader can create a toxic work environment, characterized by high levels of stress, conflict, and disengagement. This is antithetical to the principles of Conscious Leadership, which emphasize emotional intelligence, empathy, and creating a positive, inclusive work culture.

The first step in overcoming these barriers is awareness. Mindfulness practices can be particularly effective in helping you become more aware of your defensive mechanisms and emotional triggers. Once you're aware of them, you can choose to respond differently. Cognitive-behavioral techniques, such as challenging your thought patterns or reframing your perspective, can also be useful in dismantling these psychological barriers.

Defensive mechanisms and emotional triggers are significant obstacles to self-awareness and, by extension, Conscious Leadership. However, they are not insurmountable. With awareness, introspection, and the willingness to confront uncomfortable truths about ourselves, we can navigate around these barriers to become more authentic, effective, and conscious leaders.

While understanding defensive mechanisms and emotional triggers is crucial, it's equally important to build resilience and emotional agility as part of your leadership toolkit. Resilience enables you to bounce back from setbacks and maintain your leadership effectiveness, even under stress. Emotional agility, however, allows you to navigate your emotional landscape with flexibility, adapting to various challenges without getting stuck in unproductive patterns.

Building resilience often involves re-evaluating how you perceive challenges and setbacks. Instead of viewing them as threats to your self-esteem or authority, you can choose to see them as opportunities for growth and learning. This shift in perspective can mitigate the need for defensive mechanisms, as challenges become less about your ego and more about your development as a leader.

Emotional agility can be developed through practices like mindfulness, which teaches you to observe your emotions without judgment. This creates a mental space where you can choose your responses more consciously, rather than reacting out of habit or impulse. For example, if you're aware that you're feeling defensive because your authority is being questioned, you can choose to respond in a way that aligns with your values and objectives, rather than lashing out or retreating into denial.

Another strategy for enhancing emotional agility is to seek feedback from trusted colleagues or mentors. Often, we're not fully aware of our defensive mechanisms and triggers until someone else points them out. Constructive feedback can serve as a mirror, reflecting both your strengths and areas for improvement. However, for this to be effective, you need to be willing to receive and act on the feedback, which in itself requires a certain level of self-awareness and emotional regulation.

Incorporating these skills into your leadership style doesn't just benefit you; it also sets a positive example for your team. Leaders who demonstrate resilience and emotional agility create a culture where these qualities are valued and cultivated. This can lead to a more engaged, effective, and harmonious work environment, aligning closely with the principles of Conscious Leadership.

MEASURING AND EVALUATION

Recognizing and measuring Conscious Leadership can be a nuanced endeavor, as it involves both qualitative and quantitative metrics. While traditional leadership often relies on easily quantifiable measures like revenue growth or productivity rates, Conscious Leadership demands a broader set of criteria that capture its multifaceted nature.

Self-assessment is often the first step in measuring Conscious Leadership. Tools like emotional intelligence tests, 360-degree feedback, and other psychometric evaluations can provide valuable insights into a leader's level of self-awareness, empathy, and emotional regulation. However, self-assessment should be complemented by external evaluations to provide a more rounded picture.

Employee engagement surveys can be particularly useful in this regard. Questions that probe the level of trust in leadership, the openness of communication channels, and the sense of purpose among employees can offer clues about the effectiveness of a conscious leader. High levels of engagement typically correlate with effective, Conscious Leadership.

Another way to measure Conscious Leadership is by looking at employee turnover rates. Conscious leaders often create work environments where people feel valued, heard, and aligned with the organization's mission. This tends to result in lower turnover rates compared to industry averages. However, it's important to consider the context; sometimes high turnover is due to factors beyond a leader's control.

Ethical considerations can also serve as a metric. Are decisions made in an ethical manner, considering various stakeholders including employees, customers, and the community? Are there systems in place for ethical decision-making and are these systems followed consistently? An organization with a strong ethical framework that is consistently applied is likely being led by a conscious leader.

Customer satisfaction is another angle from which to measure Conscious Leadership. Leaders who are conscious of not only their internal team dynamics but also the broader impact of their organization will often prioritize customer satisfaction as a key metric. They understand that satisfied customers are often the result of a well-led, engaged team and ethical business practices.

Long-term sustainability and community engagement are additional factors that can indicate Conscious Leadership. Is the organization focused solely on short-term profits, or is there a long-term sustainability plan that takes into account environmental and social factors? Are there initiatives aimed at community engagement or social responsibility? Conscious leaders often look beyond the immediate bottom line to consider the broader impact of their organization's actions.

Measuring Conscious Leadership involves a blend of quantitative and qualitative metrics, ranging from self-assessments and employee engagement surveys to ethical frameworks and long-term sustainability plans. By taking a holistic approach to measurement, organizations can gain a more comprehensive understanding of how well they are being led and where there may be room for improvement.

BALANCING HARD AND SOFT LEADERSHIP QUALITIES

Great leaders blend **strength (hard leadership)** and **empathy (soft leadership)** to create sustainable, high-performing teams. Overemphasizing one at the expense of the other can lead to **rigidity or lack of direction.**

Hard vs. Soft Leadership Characteristics

Hard Leadership Traits	Soft Leadership Traits
Decisiveness	Active Listening
Accountability	Emotional Intelligence
Strategic Execution	Vulnerability
Clear Expectations	Adaptability
Performance-Driven	People-Centered

Framework for Balancing Hard and Soft Qualities

Leaders must adjust their approach based on **context, team dynamics, and situational needs.** A **decision-making matrix** can help leaders determine when to lead with strength versus when to engage with empathy.

Self-assessment Tool: Where Do You Stand?

- Rate yourself on a scale of 1–5 for both hard and soft leadership qualities. Identify situations where you rely too heavily on one side.
- Develop an action plan to balance both aspects.

CHALLENGES AND CRITICISMS

Conscious Leadership, like any theoretical leadership model, is open to review and criticism by those in the field. As no theory is practical and since Conscious Leadership encapsulates portions of other leadership models, the criticism and potential challenges faced by the model are important to recognize and work to counter. Concerns around idealism, industry skepticism, the abstract and complex principles behind the model, and the potential for superficial implementation are top areas of concern.

One of the most salient criticisms is the perceived idealism inherent in Conscious Leadership. Detractors argue that its focus on ethical considerations and long-term sustainability may be at odds with the immediate, bottom-line pressures that organizations often face. This criticism is particularly relevant for startups and small businesses, where short-term survival often hinges on quick returns. However, this argument assumes a zero-sum game between ethical considerations and profitability, an assumption increasingly challenged by research showing that socially responsible businesses often outperform their less responsible counterparts in the long run.

Another challenge is the abstract and complex nature of the principles that underpin Conscious Leadership. Qualities like self-awareness and authenticity, while valuable, are difficult to quantify and measure, making them less amenable to traditional performance metrics. This poses a challenge for implementation, particularly in organizations that rely heavily on data-driven decision-making. However, the rise of new metrics designed to measure social and environmental impact, as well as employee well-being, suggests that these challenges are not insurmountable.

The risk of tokenism or superficial implementation is another valid concern. As Conscious Leadership gains traction, there's a temptation for organizations to adopt its language without making substantive changes, leading to cynicism among employees. This is a challenge that goes beyond Conscious Leadership to touch on the broader issue of organizational integrity. The solution lies not in abandoning the principles of Conscious Leadership but in ensuring that they are deeply embedded in the organization's culture and practices.

The extensive demands placed on a conscious leader can also be a double-edged sword. While the ability to balance ethical considerations, emotional intelligence, and long-term strategic thinking is lauded, it can also lead to burnout and decision paralysis. This highlights the need for organizational structures that support Conscious Leadership, distributing the emotional and ethical labor across the team and providing ongoing training and support.

Skepticism from traditional business cultures presents another hurdle. Industries with deeply ingrained hierarchical models may resist the more collaborative and inclusive approach advocated by Conscious Leadership. However, as societal expectations shift and businesses face increasing pressure to demonstrate social and environmental responsibility, clinging to outdated models may pose a greater risk.

In conclusion, while Conscious Leadership faces a range of challenges and criticisms, many of these issues are not inherent flaws but rather hurdles to be overcome. They serve as valuable focal points for ongoing research and practice, offering opportunities to refine and strengthen the model. As the business landscape continues to evolve, the principles of Conscious Leadership offer not just a set of ethical guidelines but a resilient and adaptable framework for navigating the complexities of modern leadership.

CHAPTER 1 EXERCISES

Exercise 1: Self-awareness Journaling

Objective: To enhance self-awareness by reflecting on personal values, strengths, and areas for growth.

Instructions:

Spend 15 minutes at the end of each day for one week writing in a journal.

Each day, focus on a different question:

- Day 1—What values did I act upon today?
- Day 2—When did I feel most engaged and energized, and what was I doing?
- Day 3—What strengths did I utilize today, and how did they impact others?
- Day 4—What challenges did I face today, and how did I respond?
- Day 5—How did my emotions guide my actions today?
- Day 6—What did I learn about myself and others today?
- Day 7—Reflect on the past week, identifying patterns in your behavior and feelings.

Exercise 2: The Authenticity Gauge

Objective: To practice authenticity by aligning actions with core personal values.

Instructions:

Identify your top five core values.

- For one week, at the end of each day, rate on a scale of 1 to 5 how well your actions reflected these values (1 being not at all, 5 being fully).
- Reflect on moments when your actions did not align with your values. Write down the reasons and think about what you could do differently next time.

Exercise 3: Vulnerability Self-check

Objective: To embrace vulnerability by identifying and acknowledging personal limitations or mistakes.
Instructions:
Think of a recent situation where you felt vulnerable.

- Write down the specifics of the situation, your feelings, and how you reacted.
- Reflect on how your reaction was influenced by your discomfort with vulnerability.
- Consider how acknowledging your vulnerability could have led to a different outcome. Plan how you might respond in a future similar situation.

Exercise 4: Emotional Intelligence Reflection

Objective: To enhance emotional intelligence through self-regulation and empathy in interactions.
Instructions:
At the end of each day, reflect on a key interaction you had.
Ask yourself:

- How well did I listen to the other person(s)? Did I manage my emotions effectively?
- How did I demonstrate empathy?
- Write down one thing you could improve upon in future interactions to increase your emotional intelligence.

Exercise 5: The Leader's Mirror

Objective: To develop a balanced self-view by seeking and reflecting on feedback.

Instructions:

- Identify three people you trust and respect (they can be colleagues, friends, or family).
  - Ask them to provide honest feedback on your leadership qualities, particularly around self-awareness, authenticity, and emotional intelligence.
  - **Reflect on the feedback:** What surprised you? What confirmed what you already knew? How can you use this information to grow as a leader?

Exercise 6: Mindfulness Meditation

Objective: To practice mindfulness, improving presence and focus.
Instructions:

- Dedicate 10 minutes each day to mindfulness meditation.
- Find a quiet space where you won't be interrupted.
- Focus on your breath, noticing each inhale and exhale.
- When your mind wanders, gently bring your focus back to your breathing.
- Conclude each session by setting an intention to maintain mindfulness throughout the day.

their perspective and contributes constructively.

Exercise 5: Continuous Learning

Objective: To commit to ongoing personal and professional development.
Instructions:

- **Identify Growth Areas:**
  - Determine skills or knowledge you wish to enhance.

- **Set Learning Goals:**
  - Establish specific, measurable objectives for your development.

- **Pursue Development Opportunities:**
  - Engage in relevant courses, workshops, or mentorship programs.

2

Self-Awareness: The Cornerstone of Conscious Leadership

Self-Awareness is often touted as a desirable quality, but in the realm of Conscious Leadership, it takes on a pivotal role (Figure 2.1). It serves as the cornerstone, the foundational element upon which all other principles of Conscious Leadership are built. Without a deep understanding of oneself, the capacity to lead others effectively, ethically, and empathetically is significantly diminished. But why is self-awareness so crucial in leadership, and how can one cultivate it? This chapter delves into these questions, offering

Four Pillars of Self-Awareness

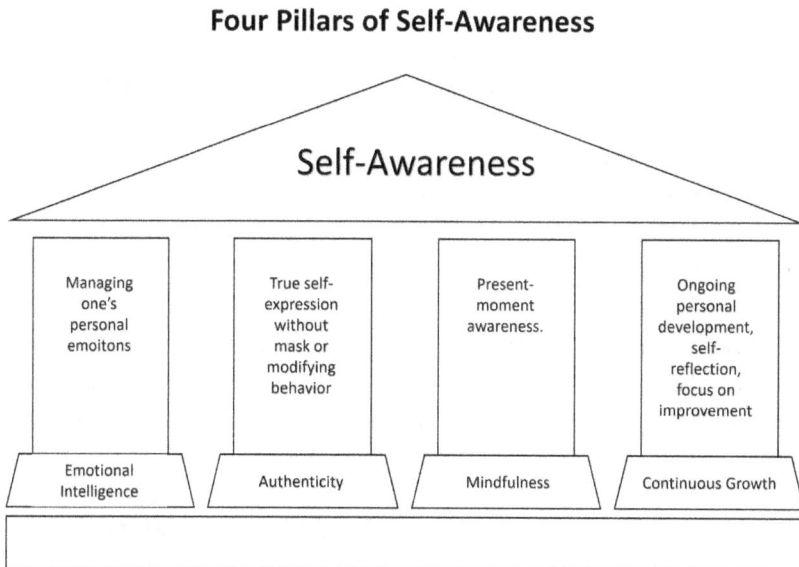

Managing one's personal emoitons	True self-expression without mask or modifying behavior	Present-moment awareness.	Ongoing personal development, self-reflection, focus on improvement
Emotional Intelligence	Authenticity	Mindfulness	Continuous Growth

FIGURE 2.1
The Relationship between Authenticity and Vulnerability.

DOI: 10.1201/9781003488705-2

both theoretical insights and practical tools for the journey toward becoming a more self-aware leader.

Emotional intelligence refers to the ability to recognize, understand, and manage one's own emotions, as well as the capacity to recognize, understand, and influence the emotions of others. In a leadership context, this means being attuned not just to what you are feeling but also to the emotional climate of your team. Leaders with high emotional intelligence can defuse conflicts more effectively, motivate team members in a way that resonates with them, and create a work environment that people are excited to be a part of. They are also better at handling stress, which is crucial in high-stakes decision-making scenarios. Emotional intelligence is not a static trait but a skill that can be developed and honed over time, much like self-awareness.

THE IMPORTANCE OF SELF-AWARENESS IN LEADERSHIP

> Know thyself
>
> *– Socrates*

Socrates' timeless wisdom urges us to delve deep into our own psyche, to understand our strengths, weaknesses, desires, and fears. It's a call to introspection, a quality that is indispensable for any leader aiming to lead consciously. The quote encapsulates the importance of self-awareness in leadership and the need for self-reflection and self-assessment in the ongoing journey to becoming a more effective leader. It serves as a reminder that the journey toward effective and Conscious Leadership starts with understanding oneself. It's a principle that has stood the test of time and continues to be relevant in the complex landscape of modern leadership.

At its core, leadership is about making decisions and influencing others. However, the quality of those decisions and the nature of that influence are profoundly affected by one's level of self-awareness. A leader who understands their own strengths and weaknesses is better equipped to deploy their skills strategically, build teams that complement their abilities, and seek development opportunities that address their shortcomings. Furthermore, self-awareness extends to emotional intelligence, enabling leaders to manage their emotions and understand the emotional currents within their teams.

This is not just a soft skill but a critical competency that impacts everything from employee engagement to the bottom line.

Cultivating self-awareness is an ongoing process that requires both introspection and feedback from others. Self-reflection involves setting aside time to consider your actions, decisions, and emotional responses. Journaling can be an effective self-reflection tool, providing a space to explore your thoughts and feelings in depth. Mindfulness practices, such as meditation, can also enhance self-awareness by training you to observe your thoughts and emotions without judgment.

Self-assessment tools offer another avenue for increasing self-awareness. Psychometric tests like the Myers-Briggs Type Indicator (MBTI) or the Emotional Intelligence Appraisal can provide valuable insights into your personality traits and emotional competencies. However, these tools should be used in conjunction with other methods, such as 360-degree feedback, where peers, subordinates, and superiors provide anonymous feedback about your performance. This multi-pronged approach ensures a more rounded understanding of yourself, mitigating the biases that can distort self-perception.

Becoming a self-aware leader is not a destination but a journey, one that requires ongoing effort and commitment. It involves not just periodic self-reflection and assessment but a willingness to act on the insights gained. This may mean seeking out professional development opportunities, engaging in coaching or mentoring relationships, or even making significant career decisions based on a newfound understanding of your values and goals.

Moreover, self-awareness is not a solitary pursuit. It's a collaborative effort that benefits from a supportive organizational culture, one that values emotional intelligence and ethical behavior. Organizations can support the development of self-aware leaders by providing training programs, creating spaces for open and honest feedback, and recognizing and rewarding self-aware behavior.

In summary, self-awareness is the cornerstone of Conscious Leadership, underpinning the ethical, emotional, and relational competencies that define this leadership style. Cultivating self-awareness is a complex but rewarding journey, one that enhances not just your effectiveness as a leader but also your well-being and personal fulfillment. By committing to this journey, you're taking the first, crucial step toward becoming a conscious leader, capable of navigating the complexities and ethical dilemmas of the modern world with integrity and compassion (Figure 2.2).

Emotional Intelligence	Authenticity
• Managing one's emotions	• True-Self Expression
Mindfulness	**Continuous Growth**
• Present Moment Awareness	• Ongoing Personal Development

Self-Awareness

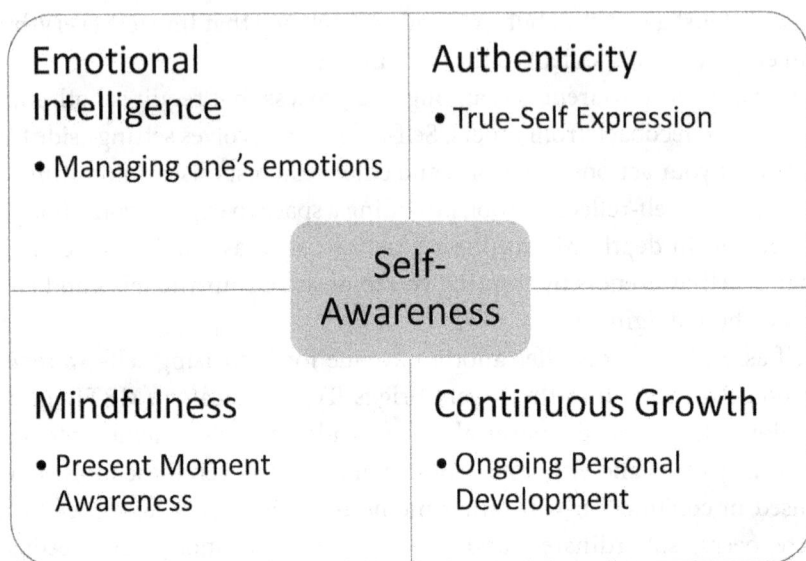

FIGURE 2.2
Four Quadrants of Self-Awareness.

THE ROLE OF EMOTIONAL REGULATION

Understanding your emotions is a crucial first step, but it's only half the battle. The ability to manage those emotions, especially in stressful or high-stakes situations, is what sets exceptional leaders apart. This skill is known as emotional regulation, a critical component of emotional intelligence and, by extension, Conscious Leadership.

Emotional regulation doesn't mean suppressing your emotions or pretending they don't exist. On the contrary, it involves acknowledging your emotional state and then deciding the most constructive way to express or channel those feelings. For instance, if a project setback triggers frustration, emotional regulation could involve taking a few deep breaths to gain composure before discussing the issue with your team. This not only helps you make more rational decisions but also sets a positive emotional tone for your team, fostering a more constructive and collaborative work environment.

The ability to regulate emotions is particularly vital in conflict resolution. Leaders are often called upon to mediate disputes or make unpopular decisions. Emotional regulation equips you to approach these situations with a level head, making it easier to find common ground or navigate complex social dynamics. It allows you to be empathetic to others' viewpoints without getting swept up in the emotional undertow, leading to more effective and sustainable solutions.

So, how can you improve your emotional regulation skills? Mindfulness practices can be incredibly effective. Techniques such as deep-breathing exercises, meditation, or even short mindfulness breaks can help you become more aware of your emotional state, giving you the space to choose how to respond rather than react impulsively. Cognitive behavioral techniques, such as challenging your own thought patterns and beliefs that may be fueling emotional volatility, can also be useful.

Another strategy is to develop a "pause button" or "Mindful Moment When you feel a strong emotion coming on, especially one that could lead to a reactive response, take a moment to pause. Use this time to breathe, reflect, and choose your response carefully. This simple act of pausing can be incredibly powerful, providing a buffer against emotional impulsivity.

Moreover, emotional regulation is not just a solo endeavor. A supportive organizational culture can play a significant role in helping leaders and team members alike manage their emotions effectively. This could involve formal training programs, mentorship opportunities, or simply fostering an open environment where people feel comfortable sharing their feelings and challenges without judgment.

Emotional regulation doesn't just impact the leader; it sets the emotional tone for the entire team or organization. Leaders who are adept at managing their emotions create a sort of emotional contagion. Team members are more likely to mirror the balanced emotional behavior of their leaders, which can lead to a more harmonious, productive work environment. This is particularly important in high-stress industries or roles where the emotional stakes are high. In such settings, the ability of a leader to remain composed can be the difference between a team that thrives and one that implodes.

Furthermore, emotional regulation contributes to ethical decision-making. When you're able to manage your emotions effectively, you're less likely to make impulsive decisions that you might later regret. This is crucial for Conscious Leadership, which places a high value on ethical considerations and the well-being of all stakeholders. A leader who can regulate their emotions is better equipped to weigh the ethical implications of their decisions, leading to outcomes that are more aligned with the principles of Conscious Leadership.

It's also worth noting that emotional regulation can enhance your personal well-being. Leaders often face high levels of stress and burnout, and the ability to manage one's emotions can act as a buffer against these pressures. This not only improves your quality of life but also makes you a more effective leader. After all, a leader who is burned out or constantly stressed is less able to guide their team effectively.

In the realm of Conscious Leadership, emotional regulation is not a stand-alone skill but is interconnected with other competencies like self-awareness, empathy, and mindfulness. For instance, the self-awareness you cultivate through mindfulness practices can make it easier to recognize when you need to regulate your emotions. Similarly, the empathy you develop through emotional intelligence can help you understand the emotional needs and responses of your team members, making it easier to navigate complex interpersonal dynamics.

In summary, emotional regulation is a key facet of emotional intelligence that has direct implications for Conscious Leadership. It's not just about understanding what you're feeling but also managing those feelings to maintain a balanced, constructive approach to leadership. By honing your emotional regulation skills, you're not only improving your own leadership capabilities but also contributing to a more emotionally intelligent, conscious organizational culture.

BARRIERS TO SELF-AWARENESS

While the journey to self-awareness is both enlightening and rewarding, it's not without its obstacles. Understanding these barriers can equip you with the tools to navigate them more effectively, enhancing your growth as a conscious leader. Here are some common impediments to self-awareness:

Cognitive Biases

Our brains are wired to take shortcuts in processing information, leading to cognitive biases that can distort self-perception. For example, confirmation bias can make us seek out and remember information that confirms our pre-existing beliefs about ourselves while ignoring evidence to the contrary. This can create a skewed sense of self that's either overly positive or negative.

Defensive Mechanisms

Often, our minds deploy defensive mechanisms like denial, projection, or rationalization to protect our self-esteem. While these mechanisms can offer short-term emotional relief, they hinder genuine self-awareness by obscuring the truth about ourselves and our actions.

Emotional Triggers

Strong emotional reactions can cloud our judgment and make objective self-assessment difficult. When triggered, people are more likely to act on impulse, making decisions that align with their emotional state rather than their true values or objectives.

Social and Cultural Conditioning

The society and culture we grow up in can impose certain norms and expectations that shape our self-perception. This external conditioning can be so ingrained that it becomes an internal barrier to understanding our authentic selves.

Fear of Vulnerability

The process of becoming self-aware often involves confronting aspects of ourselves that we'd rather not acknowledge. The fear of appearing vulnerable or weak can deter people from delving too deeply into their own psyche.

Lack of Time and Space

In today's fast-paced world, finding the time and mental space for introspection can be a challenge. The constant barrage of external stimuli leaves little room for quiet reflection, making it easy to lose touch with one's inner world.

Organizational Culture

Sometimes, the barrier to self-awareness is not individual but institutional. Organizations that prioritize results over personal growth can discourage introspection, making it difficult for leaders to cultivate self-awareness.

Understanding these barriers is the first step in overcoming them. It allows you to be more vigilant and proactive in your journey toward self-awareness. Whether it's taking steps to mitigate cognitive biases, creating a culture that encourages vulnerability, or simply setting aside time for self-reflection, recognizing these obstacles empowers you to tackle them head-on, paving the way for more authentic and effective leadership.

CHAPTER 2 EXERCISES

Exercise 1: Daily Self-reflection Practice Objective

To cultivate a habit of introspection and identify areas for personal growth.
Instructions:

- Set aside 10 minutes each evening for self-reflection.
- Reflect on the following prompts, and jot down your thoughts:
  - What decision did I make today that I am proud of.Why?
  - What was the most challenging part of my day, and how did I handle it? Did I notice any biases influencing my decisions today?
  - In what situation did I feel least comfortable, and what does that tell me?

Exercise 2: The Feedback Loop Objective

To understand how others perceive your leadership and identify blind spots.
Instructions:
Select three to five colleagues whom you trust to give honest feedback.

- Ask them to describe your leadership style and provide specific examples.
- Request both positive feedback and areas for improvement.
- Review the feedback for patterns and take note of anything surprising or unexpected.

Exercise 3: Emotional Intelligence Mapping Objective

To recognize emotional patterns and their influence on leadership behavior.
Instructions:

- For one week, track your emotional state at three different times: morning, midday, and evening.

- Record what emotions you feel, what might have triggered them, and how you reacted.
- At the end of the week, review your notes and look for patterns.
- Reflect on how your emotions may have influenced your interactions and decision-making.

Exercise 4: Strengths and Limitations Ledger Objective

To balance self-awareness by recognizing both strengths and areas for development.
   Instructions:

- Create two columns on a page: one for strengths and one for limitations.
- List out your perceived strengths and limitations in leadership.
- Next to each, write down evidence or examples that support your self-assessment.
- Consider how you might leverage your strengths more effectively and address your limitations.

Exercise 5: The Values Clarification Objective

To align personal values with leadership actions and decisions.
   Instructions:

- Write down your top five core personal values.
- For each value, describe how it currently manifests in your leadership.
- Identify any discrepancies between your values and actions.
- Develop a plan to address these gaps and more fully integrate your values into your leadership style.

Exercise 6: Mindfulness in Action Objective

To practice presence and increase self-awareness in real-time.
   Instructions:

- Choose a routine part of your day, such as a morning meeting or commute.
- Commit to being fully present during this time, observing your thoughts and emotions without judgment.

- Afterward, take a few minutes to note any insights about your inner dialogue and state of mind.
- Reflect on how this level of presence affected your perception of the event and your interaction with others.

Exercise 7: The Role Reversal Objective

To foster empathy and a deeper understanding of team dynamics.
Instructions:

- Choose a colleague and spend a day observing their interactions and trying to understand their perspective.
- At the end of the day, write a brief summary of what you believe their experiences, challenges, and motivations might be.
- Discuss your observations with the colleague to gain insights and verify your assumptions.

3

Authenticity and Vulnerability

In the intricate tapestry of Conscious Leadership, two threads stand out for their transformative power: authenticity and vulnerability. These are not mere buzzwords or fleeting trends; they are foundational elements that shape the very core of effective, Conscious Leadership. This chapter will explore the compelling influence of authenticity, the often-misunderstood strength of vulnerability, and how both can be harnessed to build trust, the cornerstone of any successful leadership endeavor (Figure 3.1).

THE POWER OF AUTHENTICITY IN LEADERSHIP

Authenticity is the act of being true to oneself, a seemingly simple concept that holds profound implications for leadership. In a world where leaders often wear masks, projecting an image they believe others want to see, authenticity is both refreshing and inspiring. When leaders are authentic, they bring their whole selves into their roles, aligning their actions with their inner values and convictions. This creates a magnetic pull, drawing people in and inspiring loyalty and commitment.

The concept of authenticity in leadership is like a multifaceted gem, each facet reflecting a different aspect of its profound impact. At its core, authenticity is about alignment—alignment between one's inner values and external actions, between words spoken and deeds done. This alignment is not just an ethical imperative; it's a powerful catalyst for change and influence. When leaders embody authenticity, they become a beacon, offering guidance and inspiration even in turbulent times. Their authenticity serves as a magnetic force that attracts others, not just earning their loyalty but inspiring a deeper level of commitment that goes beyond mere compliance to active engagement.

DOI: 10.1201/9781003488705-3

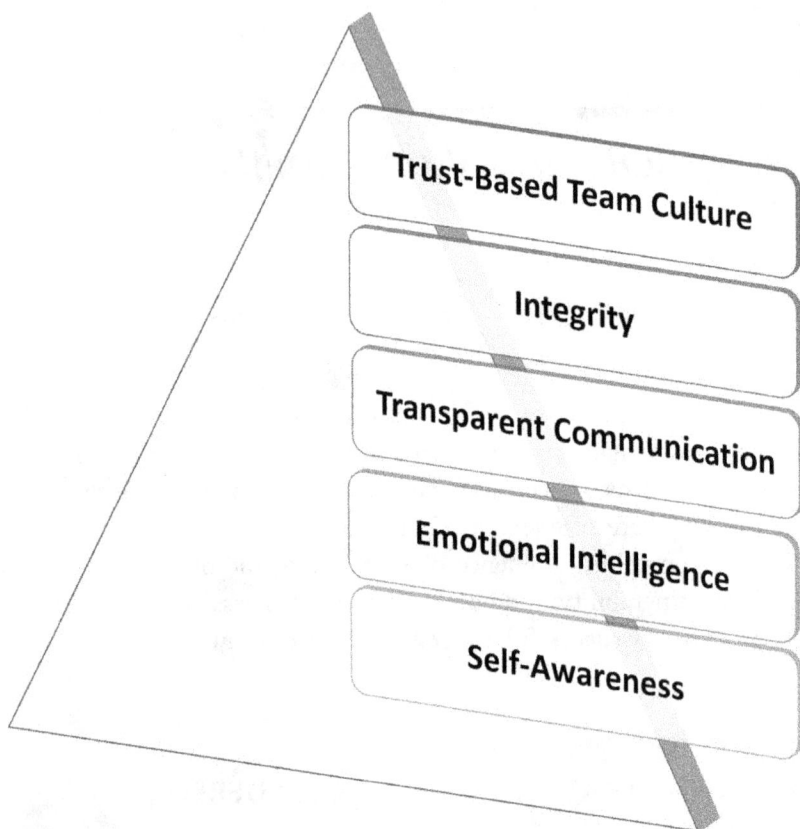

FIGURE 3.1
Authentic Leadership Pyramid.

Yet, the magnetic pull of an authentic leader is just the tip of the iceberg. Beneath the surface lies a more profound, systemic impact that can transform the very DNA of an organization. Authentic leaders serve as role models, implicitly giving permission for others to also drop their facades and be their true selves. This creates a ripple effect, leading to a culture where masks are dropped, and veils are lifted. In such an environment, the focus shifts from political maneuvering and self-preservation to collective problem-solving and innovation.

But the power of authenticity goes beyond personal magnetism. Authentic leaders create an environment where others feel free to be themselves, leading to a culture of openness and psychological safety. In such a culture, employees are more likely to share their ideas, voice their concerns, and invest their full emotional and intellectual selves in their work. The result is not just a happier workplace but also a more innovative and productive one.

Psychological safety, a term popularized by organizational behavioral scientist Amy Edmondson, plays a significant role here. When leaders are authentic, they create a psychologically safe space where team members feel valued and heard. This safety net encourages employees to take risks, such as proposing a new idea or providing honest feedback, without the fear of ridicule or reprisal. Psychological safety acts as fertile soil where creativity and innovation can flourish, leading to breakthrough solutions and driving organizational success.

Moreover, the benefits of an authentic leadership style extend beyond the immediate team or organization. In today's interconnected world, where businesses are increasingly held accountable for their social and environmental impact, authenticity can serve as a competitive advantage. Stakeholders, including customers and investors, are drawn to organizations that 'walk the talk,' that align their actions with their stated values. Authenticity, therefore, is not just an internal leadership quality but also an external marker of an organization's integrity and reliability.

In essence, the power of authenticity in leadership is transformative. It has the potential to shift the organizational culture, drive innovation, enhance stakeholder relations, and elevate the overall performance of the team or organization. It's a leadership approach for the modern world, one that recognizes that the most potent form of influence comes not from authority or coercion but from the ability to authentically connect with the hearts and minds of others.

This leadership approach also has a profound impact on employee well-being and job satisfaction. When leaders are authentic, they not only create a culture of psychological safety but also contribute to a sense of purpose and meaning in the workplace. Employees who feel that their leaders are genuine are more likely to be engaged in their work, leading to higher levels of job satisfaction and lower rates of burnout. This, in turn, has a positive impact on key performance indicators like productivity, employee retention, and even customer satisfaction.

Authenticity also has a self-reinforcing quality. When leaders are true to themselves, they find it easier to maintain a consistent leadership style, even under pressure. This consistency further strengthens the trust and credibility they have with their teams. It's a virtuous cycle: authenticity breeds trust, which in turn fosters an environment where authenticity can thrive even more.

Furthermore, authenticity in leadership is not a static quality but a dynamic, evolving one. It requires ongoing self-reflection and adaptation. The world is constantly changing, and what was authentic in one context may not be in another. This makes authenticity both challenging and exciting; it's a journey of continuous self-discovery and growth. Leaders who are committed to being authentic often find that they not only become better leaders but also more fulfilled individuals. They develop a deeper understanding of themselves, a clearer sense of their values, and a greater appreciation for the richness and complexity of human experience.

The implications of this are far-reaching, extending beyond the business world into society at large. In a world where misinformation and mistrust are rampant, the need for authentic leadership has never been greater. Authentic leaders can serve as beacons of integrity and trustworthiness, not just within their organizations but also in their broader communities. They have the potential to inspire a new social contract, one based on mutual respect, shared values, and a collective commitment to creating a better future (Figure 3.2).

The power of authenticity in leadership is multi-dimensional, affecting not just the leader but the team, the organization, and potentially, society as a whole. It's a cornerstone of Conscious Leadership, enabling leaders to forge deeper connections, drive meaningful change, and leave a lasting legacy. By embracing authenticity, leaders are not just enhancing their effectiveness; they're also contributing to a more transparent, equitable, and compassionate world.

EMBRACING VULNERABILITY AS A STRENGTH

The traditional archetype of a leader often conjures images of an unflappable, all-knowing individual who stands alone at the helm, steering the ship through

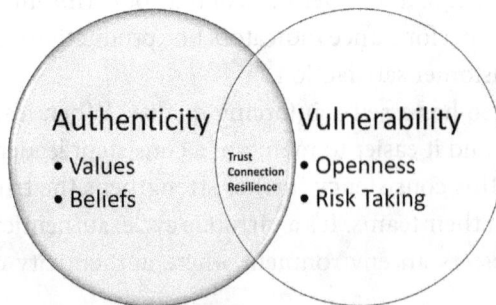

FIGURE 3.2
Relationship between Authenticity and Vulnerability.

turbulent waters without a hint of doubt or fear. This image, however, is not just unrealistic; it's also counterproductive. It perpetuates a myth of invulnerability that can be damaging both to leaders and those they lead.

Conscious leadership challenges this stereotype by recognizing the transformative power of vulnerability.

When we talk about vulnerability in the context of leadership, we're not talking about oversharing or indiscriminate emotional exposure. Rather, vulnerability in leadership is about intentional openness. It's about having the courage to show up authentically, to let go of the facade of invincibility, and to admit that you don't have all the answers. This kind of vulnerability is a conscious choice, a strategic act of emotional openness that serves a purpose: to foster trust, encourage open dialogue, and facilitate collaboration.

The act of being vulnerable as a leader accomplishes several things simultaneously. First, it humanizes you. When you admit to not knowing something or acknowledge a mistake, it shows that you are human, just like everyone else. This humanizing effect can be incredibly liberating for your team, as it dismantles the unrealistic expectations and pressures associated with the myth of the perfect leader. It sends a message that it's okay to be imperfect, which can be a relief to team members who may be struggling with their own insecurities or fear of failure.

Second, vulnerability fosters a culture of psychological safety. When leaders are willing to expose their own uncertainties or challenges, it creates a space where others feel safe to do the same. Psychological safety is a critical factor in team effectiveness, as research by organizational psychologists like Amy Edmondson has shown. In psychologically safe environments, team members are more likely to take risks, offer innovative ideas, and report errors—behaviors that are essential for learning and growth.

Third, vulnerability enhances your credibility. Paradoxically, admitting your limitations can make you more, not less, credible. When you're open about what you don't know, people are more likely to trust what you do know. Your willingness to admit ignorance or error shows intellectual honesty and integrity, qualities that are highly valued but often in short supply.

Fourth, embracing vulnerability opens the door to continuous learning and improvement. When you acknowledge your weaknesses or gaps in knowledge, you're taking the first step toward addressing them. This growth mindset, the belief that abilities and intelligence can be developed, is a key attribute of effective leaders. It's hard to improve if you're unable to acknowledge areas for growth, and it's nearly impossible to solve problems if you won't admit they exist.

Fifth, vulnerability can also be a powerful tool for conflict resolution. When conflicts arise, a vulnerable leader can de-escalate tensions by owning their part in the issue and showing a willingness to listen and change. This can encourage others to do the same, transforming a potentially adversarial situation into an opportunity for collective problem-solving.

Vulnerability is not a one-size-fits-all concept; it requires discernment and context-awareness. Being vulnerable doesn't mean indiscriminately sharing every fear, doubt, or personal issue that comes to mind. Rather, it's about choosing the right moments and the right settings in which to open up, ensuring that your vulnerability serves the greater good of the team and the objectives at hand. This level of discernment is what separates effective, conscious leaders from those who misuse or misunderstand the concept of vulnerability.

It is vital to consider the reciprocal nature of vulnerability. When a leader opens up, it often encourages team members to do the same, creating a cycle of mutual vulnerability and trust. This reciprocity is not just beneficial but essential for creating a cohesive and collaborative team. It's a two-way street that fosters a sense of shared ownership and collective responsibility. When everyone feels safe enough to contribute their authentic selves, the team becomes greater than the sum of its parts, capable of tackling challenges and achieving goals that would be unattainable for any individual acting alone.

Moreover, vulnerability has a temporal dimension; it's not just about the present moment but also about how it shapes future interactions and relationships. When leaders consistently show up as their authentic, vulnerable selves, it establishes a pattern of behavior that becomes embedded in the team's culture. This long-term impact can be transformative, setting the stage for sustained levels of high performance, employee engagement, and well-being. It creates a legacy of openness and authenticity that can endure long after individual leaders have moved on, making it a cornerstone of sustainable, Conscious Leadership.

Vulnerability can be particularly impactful in times of crisis or significant change. During such periods, the emotional stakes are high, and the need for authentic, empathetic leadership is acute. A vulnerable leader can navigate these challenging times with a level of emotional agility that is difficult to achieve through a facade of invincibility. By acknowledging the difficulties and uncertainties while also expressing a commitment to collective problem-solving, a leader can galvanize a team even when the path ahead is unclear.

Embracing vulnerability as a strength is a multifaceted endeavor that requires self-awareness, discernment, and a long-term perspective. It's a dynamic, evolving practice that can enrich your leadership in profound ways, from enhancing team dynamics and fostering innovation to navigating conflicts and leading through uncertainty. Far from being a sign of weakness, vulnerability is a hallmark of mature, effective, and Conscious Leadership. It's an indispensable tool in the modern leader's toolkit, one that holds the potential to transform not just individual leaders but entire organizations.

BUILDING TRUST THROUGH AUTHENTICITY

Trust is often cited as the most crucial element in leadership, and for a good reason. Without trust, collaboration becomes difficult, communication breaks down, and organizations struggle to achieve their objectives. Authenticity and vulnerability are key ingredients in the recipe for trust. When leaders consistently act in a manner that is aligned with their values, and when they're willing to show their human side, warts and all, they become more relatable and trustworthy.

Authenticity builds trust because it eliminates guesswork. Team members know that an authentic leader's actions will be guided by a consistent set of values, making them more predictable and reliable. Vulnerability builds trust because it invites open dialogue and fosters a sense of shared humanity. When leaders are willing to expose their own imperfections, it gives others the courage to do the same, creating a cycle of openness and trust that strengthens over time.

Authenticity and vulnerability are not optional extras but essential attributes for anyone aspiring to practice Conscious Leadership. They enrich our interactions, deepen our connections, and enable us to lead with greater impact and integrity. By embracing these qualities, we pave the way for a new kind of leadership, one rooted in self-awareness, mutual respect, and a shared commitment to creating a better, more conscious future.

CHAPTER 3 EXERCISES

Exercise 1: The Authenticity Audit

Objective: To evaluate how your actions align with your authentic self and values.

Instructions:

- Create a list of actions or decisions you made over the past week.
- Next to each action, rate how authentic it felt on a scale of 1-5 (1 being not at all authentic, 5 being completely authentic).
- For any actions rated below a 3, write down what pressures or fears may have led you to act inauthentically.
- Reflect on what changes you can make to ensure your actions align more closely with your authentic self.

Exercise 2: Vulnerability Practice

Objective: To become more comfortable with vulnerability in a safe and controlled setting.

Instructions:

- Choose a trusted colleague, friend, or mentor to share a personal challenge or failure with.
- Discuss your feelings about this vulnerability and ask for their perspective and feedback.
- **Reflect on the experience:** How did being vulnerable make you feel? What did you learn about yourself and the other person?

Exercise 3: Building Trust through Transparency

Objective: To strengthen trust with your team by practicing transparency.

Instructions:

In your next team meeting, share a mistake you've made recently and what you learned from it.

- Encourage team members to share their own experiences and what they learned.
- Discuss as a group how these insights can contribute to the team's growth and improvement.

Exercise 4: Recognizing and Overcoming Imposter Syndrome

Objective: To identify feelings of imposter syndrome and develop strategies to overcome them.

Instructions:
Reflect on recent instances where you felt like a fraud or feared being exposed as less capable than others believe you to be.

- Write down these instances, how you coped with them, and the outcomes.
- For each instance, challenge the validity of these imposter feelings and write down evidence of your competence and achievements.
- Develop affirmations or mantras to reinforce your self-confidence in moments of doubt.

Exercise 5: Exploring Personal Vulnerabilities

Objective: To identify your vulnerabilities and understand how they can be leveraged as strengths.

Instructions:
Write down three personal vulnerabilities or perceived weaknesses.

- For each, consider how it has positively impacted your leadership or how it could if embraced as a strength.
- Share these thoughts with a mentor or peer and discuss how these vulnerabilities can contribute to authentic leadership.

Exercise 6: Daily Reflection on Authenticity and Vulnerability

Objective: To reflect daily on moments of authenticity and vulnerability and their impact.

Instructions:
At the end of each day, write down at least one instance where you were either authentic or vulnerable.

- Note the context, your feelings, the reaction of others, and the outcome.
- Reflect on these instances weekly to assess how authenticity and vulnerability are influencing your leadership style and relationships.

Exercise 7: The 'Hard Conversations' Simulation

Objective: To practice having difficult conversations with authenticity and vulnerability.

Instructions:
Think of a difficult conversation you need to have or had recently.

- Role-play this conversation with a colleague or coach, focusing on being both authentic and vulnerable.
- Debrief after the role-play to discuss what went well, what was challenging, and how you might improve in real situations.

4

Mindfulness in Leadership

Mindfulness is not merely a trendy buzzword but a fundamental practice that can transform leadership styles. We explore what mindfulness is, its practical application for leaders, and its powerful impact on decision-making and stress management.

In today's fast-paced, ever-changing world, the demands on leaders are immense. Decision-making often occurs in the blink of an eye, and stress is a constant companion. It's easy to get caught up in the whirlwind of responsibilities and lose sight of the bigger picture. This is where mindfulness comes in. Mindfulness is not just a buzzword or a passing trend; it's a mental discipline that has profound implications for leadership. In this chapter, we will explore what mindfulness is, offer practical exercises for incorporating it into your leadership practice, and examine its impact on decision-making and stress management.

UNDERSTANDING MINDFULNESS

Mindfulness is the practice of being present and paying attention in a particular way: on purpose, in the present moment, and non-judgmentally. It's about being fully engaged in the here and now, rather than dwelling on the past or worrying about the future. For leaders, mindfulness offers a way to rise above the noise and chaos, providing a clearer perspective on what really matters. It enhances emotional intelligence, improves focus, and elevates cognitive function, all of which are critical leadership skills. But mindfulness is not just about individual well-being; it also has a ripple effect on your team and organization. A mindful leader serves as a role model, encouraging a culture of presence, attentiveness, and thoughtful action.

DOI: 10.1201/9781003488705-4

Mindfulness, often associated with practices like yoga and meditation, is a profound concept that extends far beyond these activities. In the context of leadership, it's a powerful tool for enhancing professional effectiveness and personal well-being.

PROFESSIONAL BENEFITS OF MINDFULNESS

Enhanced Focus and Presence: Mindfulness helps leaders stay fully engaged in the present moment. Imagine a scenario where a manager is in a crucial client meeting. By practicing mindfulness, they can actively listen to the client's needs, respond thoughtfully, and build a stronger client relationship.

Effective Communication: In team interactions, mindfulness fosters better communication. For instance, during a team brainstorming session, a mindful leader can encourage open dialogue, ensuring that every team member's perspective is heard and valued.

Stress Reduction: Leadership often involves high-pressure situations. Mindfulness equips leaders with stress-reduction techniques. In a scenario where a project faces unexpected challenges, a mindful leader can maintain composure, make rational decisions, and guide the team through adversity.

Improved Decision-Making: Mindfulness sharpens decision-making skills. In a scenario where a CEO must decide on a critical merger, mindfulness allows them to consider all factors objectively, reduce impulsive choices, and make decisions aligned with long-term goals.

Conflict Resolution: Mindful leaders are skilled in conflict resolution. In a scenario where team members have disagreements, a mindful leader can mediate the conflict, promote understanding, and guide the team toward a harmonious solution.

Empathy and Team Building: Mindfulness cultivates empathy. When a leader understands their team's perspectives and emotions, they can create a positive work environment. In a scenario where an employee faces personal challenges, a mindful leader can offer support and flexibility, fostering loyalty and motivation.

Adaptability: Leadership requires adaptability. Mindful leaders embrace change with resilience. In a scenario where a market shift impacts the business, a mindful leader can lead the team in adapting strategies swiftly.

Conflict Escalation: In a workplace scenario, a disagreement between team members can quickly escalate into a full-blown conflict when individuals react impulsively without mindfulness. Without pausing to consider their emotions and the perspectives of others, conflicts may intensify, affecting team dynamics and productivity. Mindfulness intervenes by encouraging individuals to respond calmly and thoughtfully, de-escalating conflicts and fostering more constructive discussions.

Misunderstandings: In day-to-day interactions, misunderstandings can occur when individuals don't actively listen or misinterpret verbal and non-verbal cues. For instance, during a project discussion, someone might misinterpret a colleague's tone as hostile when it was meant to be assertive. Mindfulness promotes active listening and empathy, reducing the likelihood of misunderstandings. By truly focusing on what others are saying and being open to their viewpoints, individuals can navigate conversations with greater clarity and understanding.

Communication Breakdowns: High-stress situations, such as tight project deadlines or client presentations, can lead to communication breakdowns when individuals fail to communicate effectively. Without mindfulness, stress may hinder clear communication, potentially resulting in missed deadlines or misinformed decisions. Mindfulness equips individuals with techniques to remain composed and articulate during high-pressure situations, ensuring that vital information is conveyed accurately.

By incorporating mindfulness into daily interactions, individuals can address these situational issues proactively. It enables them to respond rather than react, actively listen to others, and maintain effective communication even under stress, ultimately fostering a more harmonious and productive work environment.

PRACTICAL MINDFULNESS EXERCISES FOR LEADERS

So how can you cultivate mindfulness in your leadership practice? Here are some practical exercises to get you started:

Mindful Breathing: Take a few minutes each day to focus solely on your breath. Inhale deeply through your nose, hold for a few seconds, and exhale fully through your mouth. This simple exercise can serve as a mental "reset," helping you approach challenges with a fresh perspective.

Body Scan: Before an important meeting or decision-making session, take a few moments to mentally scan your body from head to toe. Notice any areas of tension or discomfort and consciously relax those muscles. This practice not only reduces stress but also enhances your emotional awareness, a key component of effective leadership.

Mindful Listening: During conversations, make a conscious effort to be fully present. Listen without interrupting and resist the urge to formulate your response while the other person is still speaking. This fosters better communication and builds trust, both of which are essential for effective leadership.

The process of being mindful in a day involves cultivating awareness and presence throughout your daily activities. This practice can help you manage stress, make more thoughtful decisions, and respond to challenges with logic rather than reacting emotionally.

For example, a mindful approach would take a short moment for a consistent morning routine that sets the individual reflection:

Start Your Day Mindfully: Begin by taking a few minutes for yourself in the morning. You can practice mindfulness through meditation, deep breathing, or simply by focusing on your breath and setting positive intentions for the day ahead.

Throughout the Day:

1. **Mindful Breathing:** Incorporate mindful breathing exercises into your routine. Whenever you feel stressed or overwhelmed, take a mindful minute to focus on your breath. Inhale deeply, hold for a few seconds, and then exhale slowly. This helps to calm your nervous system and brings your attention to the present moment.

2. **Mindful Eating:** During meals, pay full attention to the flavors, textures, and sensations of your food. Avoid multitasking or eating on autopilot. Mindful eating can enhance your connection to your body and improve digestion.

3. **Mindful Walking:** When you have a moment to walk, whether it's between meetings or during a break, practice mindful walking. Pay attention to each step, the feeling of your feet on the ground, and the rhythm of your walking. This can help clear your mind and reduce stress.

4. **Mindful Listening:** During conversations, give your full attention to the speaker. Listen without formulating your response in advance. This can improve your understanding of others and enhance your relationships.

Before Responding to Stressors

1. **Pause and Breathe:** When confronted with a stressor or challenging situation, pause before reacting. Take a few deep breaths to center yourself. This brief moment allows you to disengage from an immediate emotional response.
2. **Acknowledge Emotions:** Recognize your emotions without judgment. Understand that emotions are a natural part of being human, but they don't need to dictate your actions. By acknowledging your feelings, you create space for a more measured response.
3. **Logic over Emotion:** After pausing and acknowledging your emotions, consider the situation logically. What is the best course of action, given the facts? Mindfulness helps you respond rationally rather than reacting impulsively based on emotional triggers.

Impact of Emotions

Emotions have a profound impact on individuals. When left unchecked, strong emotions can lead to impulsive decisions, strained relationships, and increased stress. Mindfulness provides a tool to navigate these emotional waters more skillfully. By practicing mindfulness, you gain greater emotional intelligence, allowing you to manage your feelings effectively and respond to stressors with resilience and clarity. This not only benefits your personal well-being but also your interactions with others, fostering healthier relationships and more productive outcomes in both personal and professional spheres.

THE IMPACT OF MINDFULNESS ON DECISION-MAKING AND STRESS MANAGEMENT

Mindfulness is not just a trendy buzzword. It has tangible benefits for leaders, especially when making sound decisions and managing the inevitable stress that accompanies leadership roles.

Mindful leaders tend to make better decisions. By staying fully present and considering all available information, they can make well-informed choices. This approach also allows them to see situations from multiple perspectives, crucial in complex decision-making processes.

Leaders often face high-stress situations. Mindfulness can be a powerful tool for mitigating this stress. By staying centered and composed, leaders can navigate challenging circumstances without succumbing to anxiety or emotional reactions. The ability to remain calm and focused in times of crisis is a hallmark of a mindful leader.

Mindfulness in leadership is not merely a trend; it is a fundamental pillar of Conscious Leadership. Understanding mindfulness, practicing exercises enhancing it, and appreciating its impact on decision-making and stress management is pivotal in becoming an effective and empathetic leader. As you continue your journey toward Conscious Leadership, remember that the power of mindfulness lies in the present moment, where your leadership truly comes to life.

Expanding on the impact of emotions, it's essential to recognize that emotions can significantly influence our daily lives. They can cloud our judgment, trigger impulsive reactions, and, when unmanaged, lead to unnecessary conflicts and stress.

In stressful meetings or challenging interactions, emotions can run high, often leading to unproductive outcomes. Without mindfulness, individuals might react emotionally, saying or doing things they later regret. This can damage relationships, hinder effective communication, and impede problem-solving.

However, the mindful process introduces a powerful antidote to this emotional turbulence. By taking a mindful minute between stress-filled meetings, individuals can ground themselves in the present moment. This brief pause allows emotions to settle, preventing immediate emotional responses.

Moreover, when faced with a stressor, taking a moment before reacting allows individuals to engage their logical thinking. Instead of impulsively responding based on emotions like anger or frustration, they can analyze the situation more objectively. This leads to more thoughtful and constructive responses, ultimately enhancing problem-solving and conflict resolution.

Emotions are a natural part of being human, and they offer valuable information about our needs and concerns. However, reacting solely based on emotions can lead to misunderstandings and worsen conflicts. Mindfulness helps individuals become aware of their emotions, accepting them without judgment. This acceptance creates space between the emotional stimulus and their response, allowing for a more considered, rational reaction.

The mindful process empowers individuals to manage their emotions, navigate stressors, and respond with clarity and logic. This not only benefits their well-being but also has a ripple effect on their interactions with others, creating a more harmonious and productive environment in both personal and professional settings.

Mindfulness can be a game-changer when it comes to decision-making and stress management. By promoting a state of calm attentiveness, mindfulness allows you to assess situations more objectively, free from the distortions of emotional reactivity or cognitive biases. You become more adept at recognizing the nuances and complexities of a situation, enabling you to make decisions that are both thoughtful and effective. Moreover, mindfulness fosters emotional regulation, helping you manage stress more effectively. It equips you with the mental tools to navigate high-pressure situations without succumbing to burnout or decision fatigue.

Mindfulness is not just an optional add-on to leadership; it's a fundamental skill that enhances both personal effectiveness and organizational performance. By understanding mindfulness, practicing it through simple yet impactful exercises, and recognizing its influence on decision-making and stress management, you can elevate your leadership to a level of conscious, intentional influence. Mindfulness offers a pathway to not just surviving the challenges of leadership but thriving amidst them (Figure 4.1).

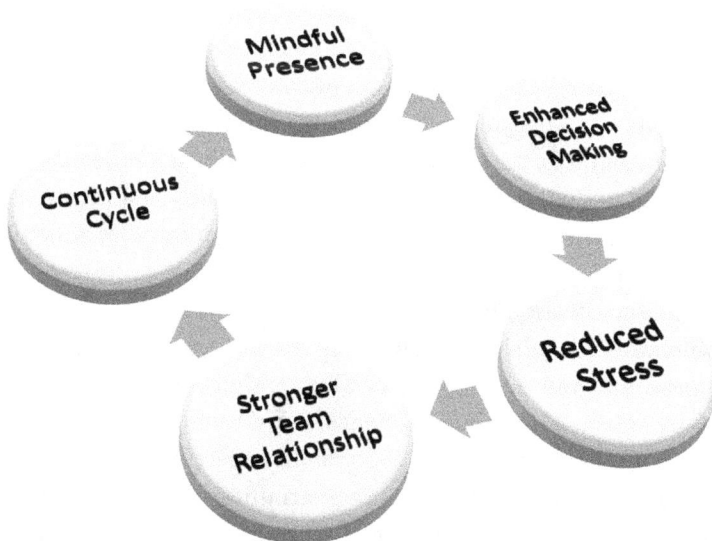

FIGURE 4.1
The Mindful Leadership Model.

PRACTICAL MINDFULNESS EXERCISES FOR LEADERS

Incorporating mindfulness into your leadership style is not a vague concept but a tangible practice that yields numerous benefits. Here, we delve into practical approaches and exercises that mindful leaders can embrace to enhance their leadership skills and overall well-being. These exercises are rooted in mindfulness principles and tailored for the modern leader.

1. **Meditation:** Meditation is the cornerstone of mindfulness practice. It involves setting aside dedicated time for focused awareness. As a leader, consider integrating meditation into your daily routine. Find a quiet space, sit comfortably, and close your eyes. Focus on your breath, inhaling and exhaling slowly. Whenever your mind wanders, gently bring your focus back to your breath. This simple yet powerful practice can enhance your ability to remain present in the midst of hectic schedules.

2. **Mindful Breathing:** Mindful breathing can be incorporated into your everyday activities. Take moments throughout your day to pause and focus on your breath. Pay attention to the sensation of your breath as it enters and leaves your body. This practice can ground you in the present moment, helping you approach tasks and interactions with a clearer mind.

3. **Deep Listening:** Effective communication is a hallmark of mindful leadership. Deep listening involves giving your full attention to the speaker, without thinking about your response. When someone is speaking to you, practice listening without judgment or interruption. Show empathy and understanding, and refrain from formulating your reply until they've finished speaking. This practice fosters trust and genuine connection within your team.

4. **Mindful Walking:** Mindful walking is an exercise in integrating mindfulness into your daily activities. During short breaks, take a walk and immerse yourself in the experience. Pay attention to the sensations in your body as you move. Feel the ground beneath your feet, the rhythm of your steps, and the environment around you. This practice can be rejuvenating, clearing your mind for better decision-making.

5. **Journaling:** Journaling is a reflective practice that helps you gain insights into your thoughts and emotions. Set aside time to write in a journal regularly. Document your experiences, challenges, and aspirations. By doing so, you can identify patterns in your thinking and

gain a deeper understanding of yourself, which is essential for mindful leadership.

6. **Mindful Meetings:** Transform your meetings into mindful gatherings. Start each meeting with a moment of silence. Encourage participants to take a few deep breaths and center themselves. During the meeting, practice active listening, encourage open dialogue, and be fully present. Mindful meetings foster a culture of collaboration and creativity.

7. **Mindful Decision-Making:** When faced with important decisions, engage in a mindful decision-making process. Take time to gather all relevant information and sit with it in a contemplative manner. Consider the implications of each choice, taking into account the perspectives of others. By approaching decision-making mindfully, you can make choices that align with your values and the best interests of your team.

8. **Gratitude Practice:** Cultivate a sense of gratitude in your leadership. Regularly express appreciation for your team's efforts and achievements. Gratitude practice not only fosters positive relationships but also reminds you of the value of the present moment.

Incorporating these practical approaches and exercises into your leadership style can be transformative. By cultivating mindfulness, you'll not only become a more effective leader but also contribute to a positive and compassionate work environment. As you develop these habits, remember that consistency and patience are key; the benefits of mindfulness become more apparent with time and practice (Figure 4.2).

Mindful Leadership	Autopilot Leadership
Deliberate Decisions Mindful leaders think carefully and reflect before making choices	**Reactive Decision** Autopilot leaders make decisions based on instinct or habit
Active Listening They engage in deep listening and respond thoughtfully to team members	**Superficial Listening** They respond automatically and don't fully understand the message
Balanced Emotions They are aware of their emotions and manage them effectively	**Triggered Emotions** They are easily overwhelmed by their emotions and react impulsively
Empathetic Approach They connect with their team on a personal level and value inclusivity.	**Detached Approach** They are disconnected from their team and prioritize their own goals
Sustainable Growth They focus on long-term goals and positive impact for everyone.	**Short Term Growth** They prioritize immediate results and neglect long-term consequences.

FIGURE 4.2
Mindful vs. Reactive Leadership.

CHAPTER 4 EXERCISES

Exercise 1: Mindful Morning Start

Objective: To begin each day with a clear and present mind.
Instructions:
Set aside 10 minutes each morning in a quiet space.

- Practice deep breathing, inhaling slowly for a count of five, holding for five, and exhaling for five.
- As you breathe, focus on the present moment and set an intention for the day.
- End the session by visualizing yourself carrying out your day's tasks with calmness and focus.

Exercise 2: Mindful Listening

Objective: To improve active listening and presence in conversations.
Instructions:
In your next conversation, focus fully on the speaker, putting aside all distractions.

- Listen to understand, not to reply. Notice when your mind starts to wander and gently bring it back to the speaker's words.
- After the conversation, reflect on what you learned and how being fully present affected the interaction.

Exercise 3: Mindfulness Bell

Objective: To create periodic reminders for mindfulness throughout the day.
Instructions:
Set a timer on your phone or computer to ring every hour.

- When it rings, take a minute to pause whatever you are doing, take a deep breath, and observe your current thoughts and emotions.
- Acknowledge and accept these feelings without judgment, then return to your task.

Exercise 4: Mindful Eating

Objective: To practice mindfulness during meals to enhance the experience and improve digestion.
Instructions:
At your next meal, remove all distractions such as electronic devices.

- Focus on the flavors, textures, and smells of your food. Chew slowly and savor each bite.
- Reflect on the process of eating, the nourishment it provides, and express gratitude for the meal.

Exercise 5: Walking Meditation

Objective: To integrate mindfulness into physical activity and refresh the mind.
Instructions:
Find a quiet place to walk, indoors or outdoors.

- As you walk, concentrate on the sensation of your feet touching the ground.
- Observe the rhythm of your steps, the feel of the air on your skin, and the sounds around you.
- If your mind wanders, gently bring your attention back to the physical sensation of walking.

Exercise 6: Body Scan for Tension Release

Objective: To become aware of physical sensations and release tension.
Instructions:
Find a comfortable place to sit or lie down.

- Close your eyes and take a few deep breaths to relax.
- Slowly scan your body from head to toe, noticing any areas of tension or discomfort.
- Visualize each tense area relaxing and releasing the tension with each exhale.

Exercise 7: Mindful Decision-Making

Objective: To apply mindfulness to the decision-making process.
  Instructions:

- Before making a decision, take a moment to center yourself with a few deep breaths.
- Consider the options before you, observing your initial reactions and thoughts.
- Reflect on the potential impacts of the decision, staying present and avoiding assumptions about the future.
- Make your decision with awareness, acknowledging the mindfulness you brought to the process.

Exercise 8: Gratitude Reflection

Objective: To cultivate a sense of gratitude and positive focus.
  Instructions:
  At the end of each day, write down three things you are grateful for.

- Reflect on why you are grateful for these things and how they impacted your day.
- Try to carry this sense of gratitude into the next day, observing how it influences your leadership and interactions

5

Empathy and Compassion

In the journey of Conscious Leadership, the path is paved with empathy and compassion. This chapter is a deep exploration of these integral elements, unravelling their role in leadership, how to cultivate compassion for both oneself and others, and inspiring insights through real-world case studies of empathetic and compassionate leaders.

THE ROLE OF EMPATHY IN LEADERSHIP

Empathy is the cornerstone of Conscious Leadership. It's the ability to step into someone else's shoes, understand their feelings, and see the world from their perspective. In the realm of leadership, empathy is not a mere soft skill; it's the driving force behind authentic connections, trust, and effective teamwork.

Empathetic leaders actively listen to their team members, acknowledge their emotions, and validate their experiences. They create a safe space for open communication and demonstrate a genuine concern for the well-being of those they lead. Empathy fosters a sense of belonging and motivates team members to bring their best selves to the table.

Empathetic leaders are not just concerned with the bottom line; they care about the personal and professional growth of their team. They appreciate the uniqueness of each individual, recognizing that diversity is a wellspring of innovation. This, in turn, creates a culture of inclusivity and appreciation.

Empathy is not merely a quality of Conscious Leadership; it is the heart and soul of it. In the realm of leadership, empathy is the capacity to understand and share the feelings of others. It goes beyond the superficial understanding of emotions; it requires a deep, heartfelt connection with the experiences and

DOI: 10.1201/9781003488705-5

perspectives of those you lead. Understanding the profound role of empathy in leadership is crucial for fostering an environment of trust, cooperation, and authentic communication.

Empathetic leaders have the remarkable ability to create authentic connections with their team members. By actively listening and showing genuine concern for the well-being of others, they build relationships based on trust and mutual respect. These connections extend beyond the professional realm and touch the personal lives of team members, creating a profound sense of belonging.

In today's diverse workplaces, empathy is a bridge that transcends differences. It allows leaders to understand and appreciate the unique backgrounds, perspectives, and challenges that each team member brings to the table. By recognizing and validating these differences, empathetic leaders foster a culture of inclusivity and equity, ensuring that every voice is heard and valued.

One of the tangible outcomes of empathy in leadership is the promotion of open communication. When team members feel that their leaders genuinely care about their thoughts, ideas, and concerns, they are more likely to speak openly and honestly. Empathetic leaders create a safe space where vulnerability is welcomed and encouraged. This open communication is a crucial component of problem-solving and innovation within the team.

Empathetic leaders not only listen to what is said but also pay attention to what is left unsaid. They pick up on nonverbal cues, emotions, and underlying needs. This nuanced understanding allows them to address issues before they escalate, leading to a more harmonious and productive work environment.

Empathy is a powerful motivator. When team members feel seen, heard, and understood, they are more motivated to give their best effort. Empathetic leaders know how to tap into the intrinsic motivations of their team members, aligning their work with their personal values and aspirations.

Furthermore, empathy plays a vital role in managing and resolving conflicts. When disputes arise, empathetic leaders can navigate these challenges with grace and sensitivity. They address the root causes of conflicts, facilitating resolution and maintaining positive relationships within the team.

Empathetic leadership builds a culture of trust and loyalty. Team members who feel that their leaders care about their well-being are more committed and dedicated to the organization's mission. They are more likely to stay with the company, reducing turnover and the associated costs.

In times of change and uncertainty, empathetic leaders provide stability and support. They acknowledge the emotional impact of change and guide their teams through transitions with empathy and compassion. This approach not only eases the process but also builds resilience within the organization.

In the tapestry of Conscious Leadership, empathy is the thread that weaves together authenticity, trust, and understanding. It is not a quality to be underestimated or overlooked. Rather, it is the foundation upon which other leadership skills are built. Empathetic leaders create an environment where individuals thrive, conflicts are resolved, and the team works together seamlessly. Through the practice of empathy, leaders become catalysts for positive change, and they inspire their teams to reach new heights of success.

CULTIVATING COMPASSION FOR SELF AND OTHERS

Compassion is empathy in action. It goes beyond understanding someone's suffering; it compels us to alleviate it. To be a compassionate leader, one must not only extend compassion to others but also cultivate it within themselves (Figure 5.1).

SELF-COMPASSION

Leaders often place tremendous demands on themselves. Self-compassion involves treating oneself with the same kindness and understanding that

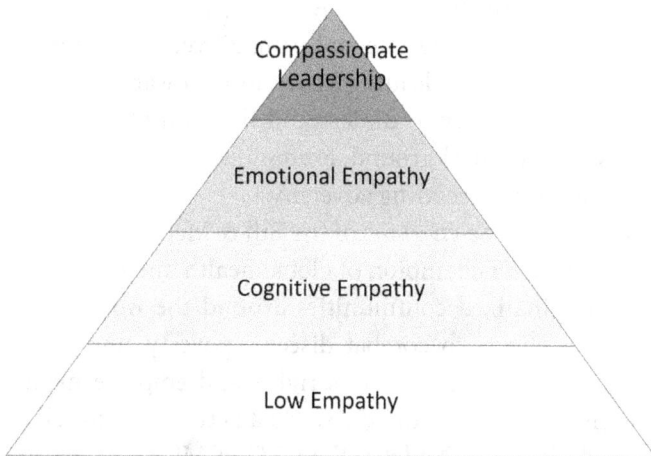

FIGURE 5.1
The Empathy-Compassion Spectrum.

they extend to others. It's acknowledging that we all make mistakes and face challenges. Self-compassion allows leaders to bounce back from setbacks, learn from failures, and maintain their emotional well-being.

COMPASSION FOR OTHERS

Compassion for team members involves not only understanding their struggles but actively supporting their growth and well-being. Compassionate leaders recognize that their team's success is interconnected with their own. They empower team members to overcome obstacles, offer guidance, and celebrate their achievements.

CASE STUDIES OF EMPATHETIC AND COMPASSIONATE LEADERS

The true impact of empathy and compassion in leadership can be witnessed through real-life examples of remarkable leaders who have embraced these qualities. Let's explore a few case studies:

1. **Nelson Mandela:** Nelson Mandela, the iconic leader of the anti-apartheid movement in South Africa, exhibited unwavering empathy and compassion. Despite enduring 27 years of imprisonment, he forgave his oppressors, leading his country toward reconciliation and democracy. His ability to understand the pain of all South Africans, regardless of their background, exemplifies the power of empathy and compassion in transcending adversity.

2. **Melinda Gates:** As a co-chair of the Bill & Melinda Gates Foundation, Melinda Gates is a champion of global health and equality. Her empathy for marginalized communities around the world has driven the foundation's efforts to combat disease, poverty, and inequality. Her compassion extends to women's rights and empowerment, reflecting her commitment to making the world a better place for all.

3. **Satya Nadella:** Satya Nadella, the CEO of Microsoft, has been recognized for his empathetic leadership style. He transformed Microsoft's culture by emphasizing empathy, humility, and a growth mindset.

Awareness
- Developing self-awareness and mindfulness to understand personal biases and emotions

Action
- Alleviate others' suffering and promote well being

Connection
- Building authentic connections with team member to create a supportive and inclusive environment

Empathy
- Cultivating the ability to put oneself in others' shoes, leading to deeper understanding and stronger relationships

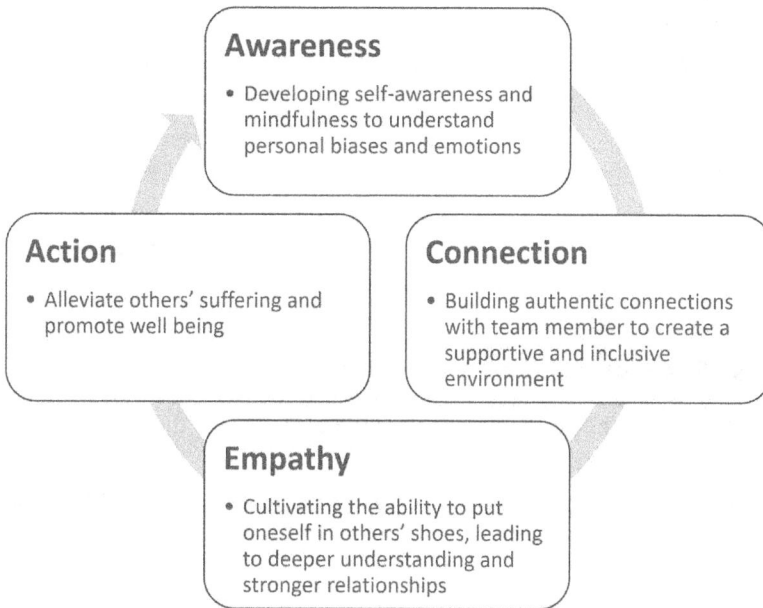

FIGURE 5.2
The Business Benefits of Empathetic Leadership.

Under his leadership, Microsoft has thrived, embracing innovation and inclusivity.

In conclusion, empathy and compassion are not mere soft virtues; they are the bedrock of Conscious Leadership. Empathy builds trust, fosters a sense of belonging, and encourages open communication. Compassion, both for oneself and others, drives leaders to support their team's growth and well-being. As we reflect on these case studies, we see that empathetic and compassionate leaders inspire positive change, showing us that Conscious Leadership is not only possible but a powerful force for good. In the chapters that follow, we will explore further dimensions of Conscious Leadership, building on the strong foundation of empathy and compassion (Figure 5.2).

CHAPTER 5 EMPATHY-BASED AWARENESS EXERCISES

Exercise 1: Empathy Mapping

Objective: To deepen understanding of team members' perspectives and experiences.

Instructions:
Select a team member and spend some time mapping out their experiences in the workplace.

- Consider their goals, challenges, and feelings they might experience daily.
- Reflect on how this new understanding can shape the way you support and interact with them.

Exercise 2: Compassionate Communication Practice

Objective: To practice and refine the art of communicating with compassion.
Instructions:
In your next team interaction, focus on expressing yourself with clarity and kindness.

- Listen to responses with the intent to understand and validate, even if you disagree.
- After the interaction, reflect on the impact of your communication style on the team dynamic.

Exercise 3: Role Reversal Scenario

Objective: To cultivate empathy by looking at situations from another person's viewpoint.
Instructions:
Think of a recent team conflict or challenge.

- Write a brief description of the situation from your perspective.
- Now, rewrite the scenario from the perspective of another person involved. Reflect on how this exercise might change your approach to the situation.

Exercise 4: Active Listening Sessions

Objective: To improve active listening skills, fostering empathy and understanding.
Instructions:
Schedule a time to have a one-on-one conversation with a team member.

- During the conversation, focus fully on what the other person is saying without planning your response.
- Ask open-ended questions to encourage them to share more about their thoughts and feelings.

Exercise 5: Compassion Meditation

Objective: To develop feelings of compassion toward oneself and others.
Instructions:
Find a quiet place and close your eyes. Begin by taking deep, calming breaths.

- Think of someone you care about and mentally send them wishes for happiness and well-being.
- Expand this compassionate feeling to include other team members, then to more challenging relationships, and finally to yourself.
- Reflect on how this meditation affects your emotional state and intentions.

Exercise 6: Journaling for Empathy Development

Objective: To use journaling as a tool to reflect on daily leadership interactions with an empathetic lens.
Instructions:
At the end of the day, write about a significant interaction with a team member.

- Describe the interaction and then reflect on the feelings and motivations that may have been behind the other person's behavior.
- Consider how you responded and how you might respond differently with this empathetic insight.

Exercise 7: The Helping Hand Challenge

Objective: To put empathy and compassion into action by helping team members.
Instructions:
Each week, identify a team member who could use support or assistance.

- Find a way to help them, whether it's through mentorship, taking something off their plate, or just lending an ear.
- Reflect on the impact of your assistance on the individual and on your relationship with them.

Exercise 8: The 'Difficult Person' Reflection

Objective: To develop empathy for individuals you find challenging to work with.

Instructions:

Think of someone you find difficult to work with and write down the qualities that challenge you.

- Reflect on what might cause them to have these qualities and how their experiences might differ from yours.
- Develop a plan for how you can interact with them more empathetically in the future.

6

The Art of Conscious Communication

In the evolving landscape of leadership, communication remains one of the most powerful instruments for influence, trust-building, and cultural coherence. It is not merely about information exchange but about the conscious act of presence, empathy, and integrity in every interaction as well. Conscious communication centers on the alignment between what is said, what is meant, and how it is perceived. When communication becomes intentional and emotionally intelligent, it fosters an atmosphere of openness, clarity, and shared purpose—especially critical in today's complex, high-stakes leadership environments.

FOUNDATIONS OF CONSCIOUS COMMUNICATION

At its foundation, conscious communication rests on several interrelated practices. Clarity and conciseness anchor the message, enabling leaders to articulate ideas in ways that eliminate unnecessary complexity. Words are chosen carefully, but so is silence, pacing, and tone. A conscious communicator doesn't simply talk—they create shared understanding. Leaders who communicate mindfully also emphasize timing: they know that the moment a message is delivered can be just as important as its content. Whether addressing performance, giving praise, or introducing change, choosing the right moment reflects emotional awareness and strategic foresight.

Equally essential is the capacity for active listening, which transforms communication from monologue into dialogue. It means more than hearing—it demands full presence, undivided attention, and an openness to truly understand the other person's intent and feeling. When leaders ask clarifying questions and offer feedback grounded in what they've heard—not

DOI: 10.1201/9781003488705-6

merely what they assume—they demonstrate respect and build trust. Active listening signals that the speaker's voice matters and invites honest, productive exchange. Over time, this cultivates psychological safety and encourages open participation.

Empathy is the emotional thread that binds effective communication. To recognize and resonate with another's experience—without attempting to fix, control, or dismiss—is a powerful act of leadership. It creates connection, reduces defensiveness, and grounds teams in mutual respect. In this way, empathy serves as both a mirror and a bridge: it reflects understanding while closing the space between people.

Communication is not just verbal. Nonverbal signals—the subtle dynamics of body language, tone, posture, eye contact, and proximity—can either reinforce or betray a message. Leadership presence often precedes speech, shaping how a message is received before a single word is spoken. An open posture, relaxed facial expression, and sustained but non-invasive eye contact can calm tension, communicate empathy, and signal receptiveness. Even a leader's spatial awareness—how they position themselves in a room or on screen—conveys influence and intention. Voice tone and cadence matter too; a steady voice under pressure builds confidence and can defuse escalating tension.

When communicating difficult truths or engaging in high-stakes conversations, conscious leaders prepare not only their talking points but also their internal emotional posture. They examine their intentions, consider the emotional context, and prioritize honesty over comfort. Using "I" statements to describe observations or concerns—rather than accusations or assumptions—helps preserve dignity while asserting clarity. The goal is not to avoid discomfort, but to navigate it respectfully. After such conversations, follow-through becomes crucial; support, feedback loops, and tangible action demonstrate that hard conversations are not isolated events but part of a process of mutual accountability and growth.

Transparency, paired with authenticity, deepens trust. When leaders speak honestly, even in uncertainty, and explain not just decisions but the reasoning behind them, they align actions with stated intentions. They don't perform clarity—they embody it. They acknowledge mistakes, admit when they don't know, and remain open to challenges. Transparency involves being upfront about challenges and limitations, sharing information freely, and inviting feedback. Leaders who model this create a ripple effect throughout the organization, fostering cultures where openness is valued and reinforced.

This kind of trust is also strengthened by storytelling—a narrative practice that connects head and heart. Stories humanize the leader, give shape to complex ideas, and offer teams a way to internalize values through lived or imagined experiences. Conscious leaders use stories to illustrate vision, confront adversity, or celebrate team growth. A mindful story—delivered with clear intent, emotional resonance, and relevance to the listener's world—can do more than any policy memo or slide deck. It inspires, it teaches, and it builds connection.

Figure 6.1, "The Leadership Communication Model," illustrates the relationship between intentional clarity, emotional presence, and nonverbal resonance. It shows that the conscious communicator doesn't just convey information—they shape experience by attending to both the content and context of every interaction. Later, Figure 6.2, "The Five Components of Conscious Communication," outlines the foundational principles of presence, empathy, transparency, adaptability, and feedback. These aren't mechanical steps but interwoven practices, guiding how leaders relate to others in every channel—verbal, physical, or digital.

COMMUNICATION IN DIGITAL AND DISTRIBUTED ENVIRONMENTS

As organizations shift increasingly toward hybrid and remote operations, conscious communication must adapt to the realities of digital environments. Unlike physical presence, digital communication lacks many of the nonverbal cues we rely on to assess emotion, nuance, or social rhythm. A flat-sounding message, a curt Slack reply, or a misinterpreted silence

FIGURE 6.1
The Leadership Communication Model.

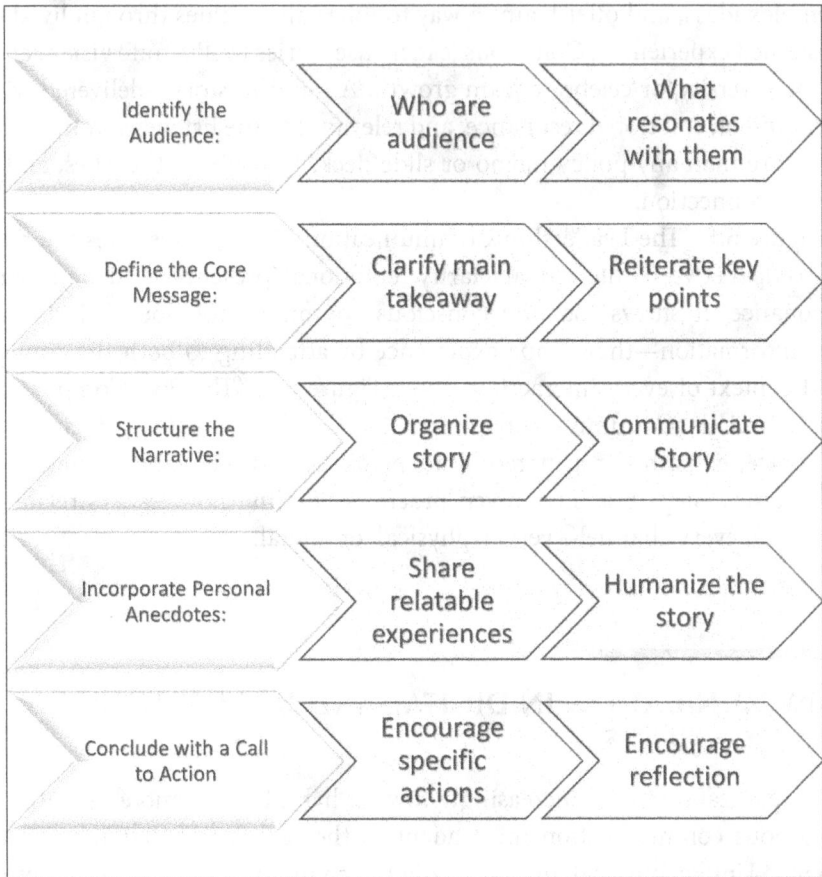

FIGURE 6.2
The Five Components of Conscious Communication.

can erode trust or spark unintended conflict. That's why mindful use of technology—what is said, when it is sent, and how it is framed—matters more than ever.

Effective digital communication involves more than writing clearly. It requires setting expectations about communication rhythms, responsiveness, and platform use. Boundaries around email hours, clarity in subject lines, and awareness of tone become leadership responsibilities. When leaders initiate regular, intentional check-ins—especially without a performance agenda—they reinforce connection and trust, allowing teams to feel seen even at a distance. Digital platforms should be tools for presence, not substitutes for it.

In virtual meetings, leadership presence comes through voice, facial expression, and structure. An engaged posture, clear vocal tone, and deliberate pauses offer presence across the screen. Leaders should invite dialogue, solicit feedback, and recognize contributions with intention. The absence of physical proximity makes space even more important—leaders must learn to hold space with focus, not just fill it with words. And when misunderstandings occur, they must be addressed promptly and empathetically, not deferred or ignored.

PRACTICING AND SUSTAINING CONSCIOUS COMMUNICATION

Even with the best intentions, communication frequently breaks down. Misunderstandings arise from a host of unseen barriers: emotional reactivity, cognitive bias, information overload, and cultural dissonance. Leaders often believe they are being clear, only to learn that their message was interpreted through a lens shaped by fear, stress, or past experience. Conscious leaders do not assume shared understanding—they work to create it.

One of the most common breakdowns stems from emotional bias. A message filtered through frustration or insecurity is likely to provoke defensiveness or withdrawal, regardless of content. Similarly, leaders under pressure may speak reactively rather than reflectively, creating ripple effects of anxiety or mistrust. Cultural misunderstandings, too, can distort intent, especially in diverse or global teams. Language, tone, and gesture vary across cultures, and leaders must recognize when interpretation gaps are rooted in difference—not defiance.

To communicate through these challenges, conscious leaders practice mindful reflection before responding. They pause. They ask clarifying questions. They seek the emotional or cultural context that might not be visible but is always present. Rather than reacting immediately to tense or ambiguous communication, they breathe, notice their assumptions, and choose a more intentional response. This approach reduces unnecessary escalation and promotes mutual understanding, even in moments of conflict.

One leader found that a simple practice—pausing to name the emotion they were experiencing before responding—dramatically improved their team's dynamics. Instead of replying abruptly to criticism or correction, they acknowledged feeling tense or uncertain and then responded with curiosity. This created a tone of safety and learning rather than defensiveness.

Similarly, naming cultural context in cross-functional teams ("I realize we may be approaching this differently based on our backgrounds") helped create dialogue rather than division.

Such moments exemplify what it means to lead with communication that is not only effective but also conscious. And because communication is ultimately a learned skill—rather than an innate talent—leaders must regularly practice and refine their communication style through active engagement and reflection.

One such reflective practice involves empathy mapping. By imagining a day in the life of a team member—what they are thinking, saying, doing, and feeling—leaders begin to understand the invisible forces shaping that person's engagement and behavior. This insight helps them tailor their words and actions with more precision and compassion.

Another method is to engage in listening exercises that strip away distraction and ego. In one such practice, two colleagues take turns speaking about a work-related experience while the other listens without interruption. Afterward, the listener summarizes what they heard and asks clarifying questions—not to debate, but to deepen understanding. Even a brief exercise like this reveals how rarely we listen without planning our reply.

Conscious leaders also embrace feedback not as critique, but as a mirror. By gathering input from several colleagues—especially those they may unconsciously overlook—they uncover patterns in their communication that either build or erode trust. This feedback, when approached with humility, becomes a tool for growth.

Shifting perspective is another powerful tool. When leaders replay a recent decision and then write out how it might have looked from a different vantage point—such as that of a junior staff member, client, or peer—they uncover assumptions or blind spots that might otherwise remain hidden.

Appreciation is no less powerful than correction. Expressing gratitude to a colleague—clearly and specifically—not only uplifts morale but reinforces values. A thank you note, an unexpected callout, or a moment of sincere recognition creates emotional momentum. Leaders who do this regularly find that trust grows faster, and conversations become more candid.

To strengthen communication presence, leaders can engage in nonverbal awareness exercises. After a meeting, they reflect on their posture, eye contact, and tone. Did their physical presence match their verbal message? Did others appear at ease or guarded? What did the silence say? Adjusting small elements—slowing down speech and maintaining more open body language—can radically change the emotional impact of a conversation.

Authentic communication—especially in moments of stress—requires courage. One leadership practice encourages individuals to identify a conversation they are tempted to avoid. Instead of rehearsing how to soften or evade the truth, they write out their honest message in clear, respectful terms. They then deliver it with vulnerability, naming their intentions. These conversations are rarely easy, but they are often transformational.

Leaders who prepare for difficult conversations by clarifying both the issue and their emotional grounding enter those exchanges with greater calm and purpose. Rather than improvising under pressure, they rehearse their words, anticipate emotional responses, and prepare empathetic framing. Afterward, they reflect on what went well and where they might improve, reinforcing conscious habits over time.

Finally, leadership presence is a practice, not a trait. Before an important interaction, leaders pause, breathe, and set an intention—"I want to be fully present, respectful, and calm." They carry this intention into the room through their posture, tone, and word choice. Afterward, they evaluate how closely their presence aligned with their intent. Over time, this practice of alignment strengthens both clarity and credibility.

Through these embodied and reflective practices, conscious communication becomes more than a set of habits. It becomes a leadership philosophy. It is how values are made visible. It is how vision is translated into shared reality. And it is how leaders invite others not just to follow but also to engage, trust, and co-create the future.

CHAPTER 6 EXERCISES

Exercise 1: Empathy Mapping

Objective: To enhance understanding and empathy toward colleagues.
   Description: Choose a colleague or team member. Imagine a day in their life.
   Task: Create a chart with quadrants: "Says," "Thinks," "Does," "Feels."
   Action: Fill each quadrant with observations and insights.
   Reflection: Consider how this changes your perception of their motivations.

Exercise 2: Active Listening Practice

Objective: To improve active listening skills.
   Description: Partner with another person for a listening exercise.

Task: Practice focused listening without interruption.
Action: Summarize and ask clarifying questions.
Reflection: Discuss the experience from both perspectives.

Exercise 3: The Feedback Mirror

Objective: To understand your communication impact.
  Description: Gather feedback from five colleagues.
  Task: Create and distribute an anonymous survey.
  Action: Analyze patterns in the feedback.
  Reflection: Develop an improvement plan.

Exercise 4: The Perspective Shift

Objective: To understand diverse viewpoints.
  Description: Analyze a recent decision.
  Task: Document your decision-making process.
  Action: Rewrite from different perspectives.
  Reflection: Compare and contrast approaches.

Exercise 5: The Gratitude Expression

Objective: To strengthen workplace connection
  Description: Identify supportive colleagues.
  Task: Write personalized thank you notes.
  Action: Deliver the messages thoughtfully.
  Reflection: Monitor relationship changes.

Exercise 6: Active Listening Role Play

Objective: To practice active, mindful listening and improve understanding in conversations.
  Instructions:

1. **Set the stage:** Find a partner (a colleague or friend) and agree that one of you will speak about a recent work-related experience or challenge for about 3 minutes, while the other will be the listener.
2. **Listen fully:** If you're the listener, focus completely on what the speaker is saying. Maintain eye contact, nod or use appropriate facial

expressions, and resist the urge to interrupt or formulate a response before they finish.

3. **Summarize and inquire:** When the speaker finishes, paraphrase what you heard them say ("So what I'm hearing is..."). Then ask a couple of open-ended or clarifying questions to make sure you understood them correctly.

4. **Reflect on the experience:** Switch roles if time permits, then discuss how it felt to be truly heard and to listen without interrupting. Consider what was challenging about staying fully present and how this level of listening might improve trust and communication in your daily leadership interactions.

Exercise 7: Non-verbal Communication Awareness

Objective: To increase awareness of body language and other non-verbal cues in order to enhance communication effectiveness.

Instructions:

1. **Observe yourself:** In your next meeting or one-on-one conversation, pay special attention to your own body language. Notice your posture (are you sitting/standing upright and open?), your facial expressions, and gestures. Make a conscious effort to align your non-verbal signals with your words (e.g., nod when listening and maintain an open, relaxed posture).

2. **Tune into others:** As you interact, also observe the other person's non-verbal cues. Are they engaged and making eye contact, or do they appear distracted or tense? Take note of their tone of voice and posture to better understand their emotional state and level of comfort with the discussion.

3. **Adjust and align:** If you notice any mismatch between what is being said and the non-verbal signals (for instance, someone says "everything is fine" but has a stiff posture or frown), gently acknowledge it ("I notice you seem concerned...") or adjust your approach. Likewise, ensure your tone and expressions match the intent of your message (e.g., conveying empathy when discussing a tough issue).

4. **Reflect on insights:** After the interaction, reflect on how being mindful of non-verbal communication changed your understanding. What did you learn about the other person's feelings or your own habits by watching body language? Identify one adjustment you can make in your non-verbal communication moving forward (such as making

better eye contact or adopting a calmer tone) to strengthen your leadership presence.

Exercise 8: Authentic Communication Challenge

Objective: To practice transparency and authenticity in your messaging, building trust through honest communication.

   Instructions:

1. **Identify an opportunity for honesty:** Think of an upcoming communication where you might usually be inclined to sugarcoat the message or hold back your true thoughts. It could be giving feedback to a team member, addressing a team about a new change, or sharing your perspective in a meeting.
2. **Plan your message with authenticity:** Take a few minutes to outline what you really need or want to convey. Craft your message to be truthful and clear while remaining respectful and constructive. For example, if giving feedback, focus on the facts of the situation and your genuine feelings or concerns, phrased respectfully. If discussing a challenge or mistake, speak to what genuinely happened and what you learned, rather than burying or glossing over it.
3. **Communicate openly:** Deliver your message in person or in writing, sticking to the authentic outline you prepared. As you do so, maintain a sincere tone and steady eye contact (if in person), signaling that you mean what you say. You might preface the conversation with, "Iommlike to be candid with you about this," to set a tone of transparency.
4. **Reflect on the outcome:** Afterward, consider how it felt to communicate more openly than usual. How did the person or audience respond? Note any differences in the level of trust or understanding that resulted. Reflect on what this experience teaches about authenticity in leadership communication and how you can continue to be transparent and genuine, even when the conversations are challenging.

Exercise 9: Difficult Conversation Preparation

Objective: To develop a strategy for handling a difficult conversation effectively and empathetically.

Instructions:

1. **Choose a tough topic:** Identify a difficult conversation you have been avoiding or need to engage in. It might be addressing a performance issue with an employee, confronting a teammate about a disagreement, or delivering unwelcome news.
2. Clearly define the core issue you need to talk about.
3. **Plan your key points:** Write down the main points you want to communicate during this conversation. Use clear, factual statements and In language to express your perspective without blame (e.g., "I noticed deadlines have been missed..." or "I feel concerned about..."). Be specific about the outcomes you desire or any changes you'd like to see, so your message is constructive and goal-oriented.
4. **Anticipate their perspective:** Put yourself in the other person's shoes and consider how they might feel or react when you engage in this discussion. List out possible reactions or concerns they might have. Prepare to acknowledge their feelings ("I understand this is difficult to hear...") and think of empathetic responses to show you respect their point of view, even if you have to deliver tough feedback.
5. **Rehearse calmly:** If possible, practice the conversation before actually having it. You can role-play with a trusted colleague or even speak in front of a mirror. Pay attention to staying calm and keeping your tone respectful and steady, even if you imagine the other person becoming defensive or emotional. This rehearsal will help you remain centered when the real conversation happens.
6. **Initiate and reflect:** Schedule and conduct the difficult conversation using your plan as a guide. Afterward, reflect on what went well and what was challenging. Did your preparation help you stay focused and compassionate? How did the other person respond, and what might you adjust in the future? By analyzing the experience, you'll refine your ability to handle difficult conversations with greater confidence and care next time.

Exercise 10: Leadership Presence Practice

Objective: To strengthen your leadership presence by being mindful of how you show up and communicate in a professional setting.

Instructions:

1. **Center yourself before communicating:** Prior to your next important meeting, presentation, or conversation, take 2–3 minutes to prepare your presence. Sit or stand quietly and take a few deep breaths to ground yourself. Set a clear intention for how you want to present yourself—for example, "In this meeting, I will be calm, confident, and fully attentive."

2. **Demonstrate engaged body language:** As the interaction begins, consciously adopt an open and confident posture. Keep your back straight and shoulders relaxed. Use eye contact to connect with others, and nod or use appropriate facial expressions to show you're engaged. Avoid nervous habits (fidgeting, looking at your phone, etc.) so that you appear focused and composed.

3. **Communicate with clarity and calm:** Pay attention to your voice and pace. Speak clearly, loud enough to be heard, and at a measured pace—not rushed. Pause briefly to gather your thoughts if needed instead of filling every silence with words. This calm pacing and clear articulation will convey confidence and give more weight to what you say.

4. **Reflect and adjust:** After the meeting or conversation, take a moment to reflect on your presence. Did you remain present and project the leadership qualities you intended (calm, confidence, empathy, etc.)? How did others react—did they seem receptive and engaged? Identify one aspect of your presence you felt good about, and one aspect to improve (perhaps you noticed your posture slouched at times or that you could listen more before speaking). Carry these insights forward and use them to continue refining your leadership presence in every interaction.

7

Servant Leadership vs. Conscious Leadership: A Comparative Study

A leader is best when people barely know he exists, when his work is done, his aim fulfilled, they will say: we did it ourselves.

– Lao Tzu

FOUNDATIONS OF SERVANT LEADERSHIP

Servant Leadership, a term coined by Robert K. Greenleaf in the 1970s, is a leadership philosophy that inverts the conventional leadership model. It emphasizes the leader's role as a servant first, prioritizing the needs of employees and the community before considering their own. The foundation of Servant Leadership lies in the desire to serve and the commitment to lead. This approach is characterized by a focus on collaboration, trust, empathy, and the ethical use of power. The servant leader's primary goal is to enhance the growth and well-being of people and the communities to which they belong.

Servant Leadership is grounded in the belief that the most effective leaders strive to serve others, rather than accrue power or take control. This philosophy is deeply rooted in personal integrity and leads to a leadership approach that is caring, participative, and empowering. Servant leaders are often seen as stewards who hold their organization in trust for the greater good of society.

DOI: 10.1201/9781003488705-7

SIMILARITIES AND DIFFERENCES BETWEEN SERVANT AND CONSCIOUS LEADERSHIP

While Servant and Conscious Leadership share common ground in their focus on ethical, people-centered leadership, there are distinct differences between the two. Both leadership styles emphasize empathy, listening, and the ethical use of power. They prioritize the well-being and development of their team members and believe in leading by example.

However, Conscious Leadership differs in its broader scope. While Servant Leadership focuses primarily on serving others, Conscious Leadership includes a more holistic view of the leader's role. It not only involves serving others but also includes self-awareness, mindfulness, and an understanding of the interconnectedness of all stakeholders. Conscious leaders are aware of their own values and behaviors and understand how these impact their decision-making and leadership style.

Another key difference is the approach to decision-making. Servant leaders may prioritize the immediate needs and well-being of their team members, sometimes at the expense of broader organizational goals. In contrast, conscious leaders strive to balance the needs of all stakeholders, including employees, customers, and the community, while also considering the long-term sustainability of their decisions.

In the intricate world of leadership theories, Servant Leadership and Conscious Leadership stand out as two philosophies that have significantly influenced modern management practices. While they share some common ground, they also diverge in key areas. This essay delves into the similarities and differences between these two leadership styles, offering insights into how they can be integrated into a cohesive leadership approach.

At their core, both Servant and Conscious Leadership are grounded in a deep sense of ethical responsibility and a commitment to the well-being of others. They prioritize the needs and development of team members, fostering environments where individuals feel valued and empowered.

One of the primary similarities is their focus on empathy. Both leadership styles emphasize the importance of understanding and addressing the emotional and professional needs of team members. This empathetic approach leads to stronger, more cohesive teams and a more positive workplace culture.

Another similarity lies in their commitment to ethical decision-making. Servant and conscious leaders are guided by a strong moral compass, making decisions that benefit not only their organization but also their wider communities. This ethical stance builds trust and respect, both within the team and with external stakeholders.

Both leadership styles also value self-awareness. Leaders who practice either philosophy are encouraged to engage in self-reflection, understanding their strengths and weaknesses, and how their actions affect others. This introspection leads to more authentic and effective leadership.

Despite these similarities, there are distinct differences between Servant and Conscious Leadership. Servant Leadership, as the name suggests, emphasizes the leader's role as a servant first. This approach is deeply rooted in the desire to serve others, with the leader often putting the needs of their team members above their own. The servant leader's primary goal is to enhance the growth and well-being of their team and the communities they serve.

Conscious Leadership, however, while also focusing on the well-being of others, takes a more holistic approach. It not only involves serving others but also includes a greater emphasis on self-awareness, mindfulness, and the interconnectedness of all stakeholders. Conscious leaders are aware of the broader impact of their decisions, striving to balance the needs of employees, customers, and the community while also considering the long-term sustainability of their actions.

Another key difference is in the approach to power and authority. Servant leaders often downplay their power, focusing instead on empowering their team members. Conscious leaders, while also empowering their team, are more likely to use their authority to drive change and influence broader organizational goals.

While Servant and Conscious Leadership have distinct characteristics, they also share important similarities. Both prioritize empathy, ethical decision-making, and the well-being of others.

However, they differ in their emphasis on the role of the leader and the use of power and authority. By understanding and integrating these two approaches, leaders can develop a style that is not only effective but also deeply rooted in ethical and compassionate principles. This integration can lead to a leadership approach that is adaptable, thoughtful, and truly transformative.

INTEGRATING SERVANT LEADERSHIP PRACTICES INTO CONSCIOUS LEADERSHIP

Integrating Servant Leadership practices into Conscious Leadership can create a powerful, holistic approach to leadership. By adopting the Servant Leadership focus on empathy, active listening, and community building, and combining it with the self-awareness and mindfulness of Conscious Leadership, leaders can develop a more nuanced and effective leadership style.

This integration involves adopting a servant leader's focus on the growth and well-being of people and communities while maintaining the conscious leader's awareness of the broader impact of their actions. It means not only serving the needs of the team but also considering the long-term implications of decisions on all stakeholders.

Leaders can integrate these practices by focusing on personal development, fostering a culture of open communication and feedback, and ensuring that their actions align with their values and the needs of their team and community (Figure 7.1).

CASE STUDIES COMPARING SERVANT AND CONSCIOUS LEADERS

Examining real-life examples of servant and conscious leaders can provide valuable insights into the practical application of these theories. For instance, a case study of a servant leader might focus on how their emphasis on employee well-being led to high team morale and loyalty, but perhaps at the cost of more aggressive business strategies. In contrast, a case study of a conscious leader might demonstrate how their balanced approach to stakeholder needs led to sustainable business practices and long-term success, though it required difficult trade-offs and a strong focus on personal development.

Southwest Airlines and Herb Kelleher

Herb Kelleher, the co-founder of Southwest Airlines, is widely celebrated for his distinctive approach to leadership, particularly Servant Leadership,

Transformational	Conscious Leadership
Vision and Goals: Focuses on inspiring change and innovation.	Emphasizes awareness and ethical considerations.
Approach to Change: Encourages risk-taking and challenging the status quo.	Promotes mindful decision-making and sustainability.
Relationship with Team: Motivates through vision and charisma.	Builds trust through authenticity and empathy.

FIGURE 7.1
Transformational vs. Conscious Leadership.

which became a cornerstone in the airline's unprecedented success and the cultivation of its unique corporate culture. Servant Leadership, a term coined by Robert K. Greenleaf, focuses on the leader serving their team, as opposed to the team serving the leader. This approach emphasizes the growth and well-being of people and the communities to which they belong.

Kelleher's leadership style was characterized by a deep commitment to employee satisfaction and customer service. He believed that a happy, well-cared-for workforce would naturally lead to high-quality customer service. This philosophy was not just theoretical but was deeply ingrained in the operational strategies and corporate ethos of Southwest Airlines.

One of the key elements of Kelleher's approach was his personal involvement and genuine interest in his employees' welfare. He was known for remembering names, participating in frontline work, and creating a family-like atmosphere within the company. This approach not only motivated employees but also fostered a sense of loyalty and commitment to the company's vision.

The impact of this leadership style was profound on Southwest's corporate culture. The airline became known for its informal, fun, and friendly atmosphere, which was a direct reflection of Kelleher's personality. This unique culture not only set Southwest apart from its competitors but also became a key factor in its operational efficiency and profitability. Employees were more willing to go the extra mile, leading to better customer service and lower turnover rates, which are significant cost factors in the airline industry.

Moreover, Kelleher's focus on simplicity and efficiency in operations, such as using a single model of aircraft (Boeing 737), also mirrored his no-nonsense approach to leadership. This decision significantly reduced costs related to maintenance, training, and operations, directly impacting the bottom line.

However, it's important to note that while Kelleher's Servant Leadership style was a key contributor to Southwest's success, it was also complemented by a solid business strategy. The airline focused on point-to-point flights, avoiding the traditional hub-and-spoke system used by other airlines, which allowed for quick turnaround times and more efficient use of aircraft.

The Servant Leadership approach Herb leveraged at Southwest Airlines demonstrates the power of a people-centered leadership philosophy. By prioritizing employee satisfaction and customer service, Kelleher not only created a strong and unique corporate culture but also laid the foundation for operational efficiency and financial success. His legacy serves as a compelling case study for the transformative potential of Servant Leadership in corporate settings.

Satya Nadella at Microsoft

Satya Nadella's tenure as CEO of Microsoft marks a significant transformation in the company's history, characterized by a shift toward a more empathetic, growth-minded, and Conscious Leadership style. This case study examines the key aspects of Nadella's leadership and how they have impacted Microsoft's culture and business performance.

Before Nadella's appointment as CEO in 2014, Microsoft was grappling with various challenges, including a declining market share in key areas and a perceived lack of innovation. The company was known for its aggressive and competitive culture, which, while successful in the past, was becoming increasingly out of step with the evolving tech industry.

Nadella's leadership style is starkly different from his predecessors. His approach is deeply rooted in empathy, influenced by personal experiences and a belief in the growth mindset, a concept popularized by psychologist Carol Dweck. This mindset suggests that abilities and intelligence can be developed through dedication and hard work (Figure 7.2).

One of Nadella's first initiatives was to shift the company culture from a "know-it-all" to a "learn-it-all" philosophy. This meant encouraging curiosity, continuous learning, and an openness to change. This cultural shift

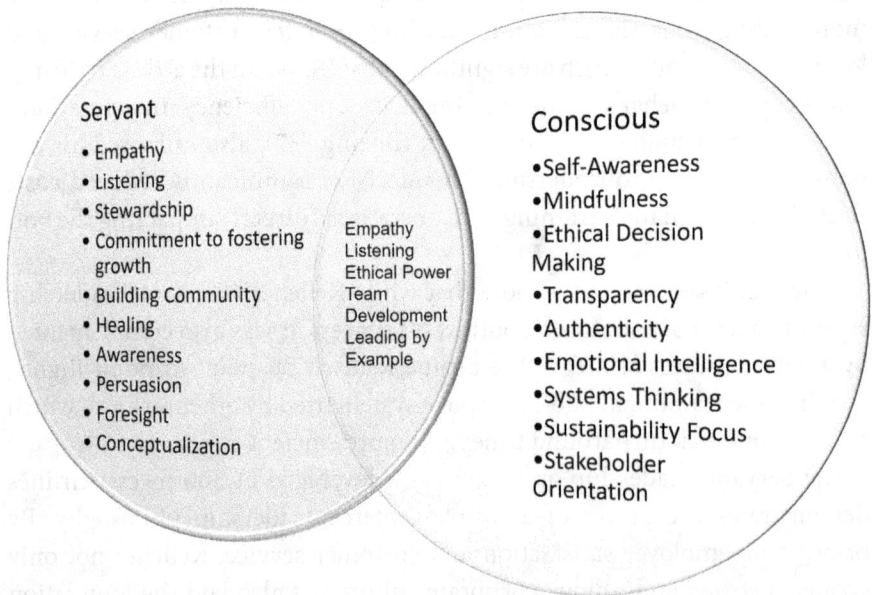

Servant
- Empathy
- Listening
- Stewardship
- Commitment to fostering growth
- Building Community
- Healing
- Awareness
- Persuasion
- Foresight
- Conceptualization

Empathy
Listening
Ethical Power
Team
Development
Leading by
Example

Conscious
- Self-Awareness
- Mindfulness
- Ethical Decision Making
- Transparency
- Authenticity
- Emotional Intelligence
- Systems Thinking
- Sustainability Focus
- Stakeholder Orientation

FIGURE 7.2
The Overlap between Servant and Conscious Leadership.

was vital in fostering innovation and agility within Microsoft, allowing it to become more responsive to market changes and customer needs.

Nadella emphasized the importance of teamwork and collaboration, moving away from the internal competition that had previously characterized Microsoft's work environment. He encouraged different departments to work together toward common goals, fostering a more unified and productive workforce.

Under Nadella, Microsoft realigned its business strategy to focus more on cloud computing and AI, recognizing the decline in traditional revenue streams like Windows and Office products.

This shift not only rejuvenated the company's product line but also positioned Microsoft as a leader in these emerging technology sectors.

The impact of Nadella's leadership on Microsoft's business performance has been remarkable. The company has seen a significant increase in its stock price and market capitalization, becoming one of the most valuable companies in the world. This financial success is a testament to the effectiveness of Nadella's leadership style and strategic decisions.

Nadella's empathetic leadership has also positively impacted employee engagement and satisfaction. By fostering a more inclusive and supportive work environment, he has improved morale and reduced turnover rates, which is crucial in the competitive tech industry.

Satya Nadella's leadership of Microsoft showcases the power of empathetic and growth-minded leadership in transforming a global tech giant. His focus on culture, collaboration, and strategic realignment has not only revitalized the company's image and product offerings but also significantly improved its financial performance. Nadella's tenure at Microsoft serves as a compelling example of how Conscious Leadership can drive successful organizational change and growth.

Patagonia and Yvon Chouinard

Patagonia, under the leadership of founder Yvon Chouinard, presents a compelling case study of how a company can integrate Conscious Leadership principles with a steadfast commitment to environmental sustainability and ethical business practices. This integration has not only defined the brand's identity but also significantly influenced its operations and business model.

Patagonia, founded by Yvon Chouinard in 1973, started as a small company that made tools for climbers. Over the years, it has evolved into a globally recognized outdoor apparel company. From its inception, Patagonia has been committed to environmental sustainability, which is deeply rooted in Chouinard's personal beliefs and experiences as an avid climber and environmentalist.

Yvon Chouinard's leadership style is a blend of minimalism, environmental activism, and practical business sense. He advocates for "responsible business," which means doing good for the planet while still making a profit. This philosophy is deeply embedded in the company's culture, influencing every aspect of its operations, from product design to supply chain management.

Patagonia's commitment to environmental sustainability is evident in several key areas:

Product Design and Materials: Patagonia prioritizes the use of recycled and environmentally friendly materials. The company has invested in developing new sustainable materials and has been a pioneer in using organic cotton and recycled polyester.

Supply Chain Transparency: The company maintains high standards for its supply chain, ensuring fair labor practices and minimal environmental impact. They openly share their supply chain practices, promoting transparency in an industry often criticized for opaque operations.

Environmental Advocacy: Patagonia actively participates in environmental advocacy, dedicating time, resources, and a portion of its profits to environmental causes. The company's activism ranges from supporting grassroots organizations to involving itself in national environmental campaigns.

Patagonia's business practices reflect a strong ethical stance:

Fair Trade and Labor Practices: The company is committed to fair labor practices, ensuring that workers in its supply chain are treated ethically and paid fairly.

Reducing Carbon Footprint: Patagonia continually strives to reduce its carbon footprint, implementing various measures such as using renewable energy sources and optimizing logistics to minimize environmental impact.

Patagonia's approach has had a profound impact on its brand and operations:

Brand Loyalty and Reputation: The company's commitment to sustainability and ethics has fostered strong brand loyalty among customers who share these values. Patagonia is often cited as a model for sustainable business practices, enhancing its reputation.

Business Performance: Despite its unconventional approach, Patagonia has seen strong business performance. The brand's authenticity and commitment to its values have attracted a dedicated customer base.

Innovation: The focus on sustainability has driven Patagonia to innovate, both in its products and business model. Initiatives like the "Worn Wear" program, which encourages repairing and recycling clothing, demonstrate innovative approaches to sustainable business.

Patagonia, under Yvon Chouinard, stands as a prime example of how a company can successfully integrate Conscious Leadership with a commitment to environmental sustainability and ethical business practices. This approach has not only positively influenced Patagonia's brand and operations but has also set a benchmark in the industry for responsible business practices.

Chouinard's vision and leadership have shown that profitability and sustainability can coexist, challenging traditional business models and inspiring a new generation of environmentally conscious enterprises.

Starbucks and Howard Schultz

Howard Schultz's leadership at Starbucks offers a rich case study in combining aspects of Servant and Conscious Leadership, particularly evident in the company's approach to employee welfare, customer engagement, and corporate social responsibility (CSR) initiatives. Schultz, who led Starbucks from 1986 to 2000 and then again from 2008 to 2017, played a pivotal role in shaping the company's ethos and operations.

Servant Leadership, as characterized by Robert K. Greenleaf, focuses on the leader serving their team. Schultz's application of this principle is most apparent in his approach to employee welfare:

"Partners" Philosophy: Schultz referred to employees as "partners," reflecting his belief in the value and dignity of each employee. This philosophy fostered a sense of belonging and respect among the workforce.

Employee Benefits: Under Schultz's leadership, Starbucks became known for offering comprehensive benefits to both full-time and part-time employees, including health insurance, stock options (Bean Stock program), and tuition reimbursement through the Starbucks College Achievement Plan. These benefits are not common in the retail sector and demonstrate a genuine commitment to employee welfare.

Inclusivity and Growth: Schultz encouraged an inclusive culture and internal growth opportunities, allowing employees to advance within the company. This approach not only improved employee satisfaction but also reduced turnover rates.

Conscious Leadership involves being aware of the company's role and impact on all stakeholders, including customers. Schultz's strategies in customer engagement reflect this:

Customer Experience: Schultz emphasized the importance of the customer experience at Starbucks. He envisioned Starbucks stores as a "third place" between work and home, focusing on creating a welcoming and comfortable environment.

Feedback and Innovation: Under Schultz, Starbucks consistently sought customer feedback and used it to innovate and improve its products and services. This approach helped the company to stay relevant and responsive to changing consumer preferences.

Schultz's leadership also extended to robust CSR initiatives, aligning with both Servant and Conscious Leadership principles:

Ethical Sourcing: Starbucks committed to ethical sourcing of coffee through its Coffee and Farmer Equity (C.A.F.E.) Practices, ensuring that coffee is grown using sustainable methods and that farmers are treated fairly.

Environmental Stewardship: The company has made efforts to reduce its environmental footprint, including initiatives to reduce waste and promote recycling.

Community Engagement: Starbucks has engaged in various community service and development projects. Schultz's vision extended to social issues, with Starbucks participating in initiatives addressing community challenges such as youth unemployment, homelessness, and veteran support.

The integration of Servant and Conscious Leadership principles under Schultz's tenure profoundly impacted Starbucks' culture and business performance:

Brand Identity and Loyalty: Schultz's leadership helped shape Starbucks' identity as a socially responsible and employee-friendly company, which strengthened customer and employee loyalty.

Financial Success: Despite the high costs associated with extensive employee benefits and CSR initiatives, Starbucks experienced significant growth and profitability under Schultz's leadership, demonstrating that a business can be both socially responsible and financially successful.

Howard Schultz's leadership at Starbucks serves as a prime example of how Servant and Conscious Leadership principles can be effectively integrated into a company's operations. His focus on employee welfare, customer engagement, and CSR initiatives not only positively shaped Starbucks' corporate culture but also contributed significantly to its commercial success and reputation as a socially responsible corporation. Schultz's leadership approach highlights the potential of ethical and people-centered business practices in building a successful and sustainable brand.

Mary Barra at General Motors

Mary Barra's tenure as the CEO of General Motors (GM) presents a significant case study in modern leadership, particularly in her approach to navigating the company through crises, her commitment to innovation and sustainability, and the manifestation of both Servant and Conscious Leadership elements in her management style.

Mary Barra became the CEO of General Motors in 2014, marking her as the first female leader of a major global automaker. Her ascent to this position came at a time when the automotive industry was facing numerous challenges, including technological disruptions, increasing competition, and a pressing need for sustainability.

Barra's leadership was immediately tested by significant challenges, most notably the ignition switch safety crisis that came to light shortly after she assumed the CEO role. Her response to this crisis showcased her capabilities:

Transparency and Responsibility: Barra adopted a transparent approach, openly acknowledging the company's mistakes. She testified before Congress, issued public apologies, and met with victims' families, demonstrating accountability and empathy.

Decisive Action: Under her leadership, GM initiated a comprehensive safety review, leading to numerous recalls and the establishment of a compensation fund for victims. These actions, although costly, were crucial in rebuilding trust and credibility.

Barra's vision for GM heavily emphasized innovation and sustainability, key areas where her leadership brought significant transformation:

Electrification of Vehicles: Barra has been a strong advocate for electric vehicles (EVs). Under her leadership, GM committed to launching multiple new electric models and announced significant investments in EV technology, positioning GM as a leader in the industry's shift toward electrification.

Autonomous Vehicles: Recognizing the potential of autonomous technology, Barra directed GM's investment in self-driving technology, including the acquisition of Cruise Automation, a self-driving car startup.

Barra's leadership style reflects aspects of both Servant and Conscious Leadership:

Employee Focus: Consistent with Servant Leadership principles, Barra is known for her employee-centric approach. She encourages open communication, empowers her team members, and is committed to developing their skills and careers.

Long-Term Vision and Stakeholder Consideration: True to the tenets of Conscious Leadership, Barra's decisions reflect a deep consideration of all stakeholders, including employees, customers, shareholders, and the environment. Her strategic choices demonstrate a balance between immediate business needs and long-term societal impacts.

The impact of Barra's leadership on GM's culture and business performance has been notable:

Cultural Shift: Barra has worked toward creating a more inclusive and diverse work environment. Her leadership has been instrumental in breaking down silos within GM, fostering a culture of collaboration and innovation.

Market Positioning: Despite the challenges, GM has maintained a strong position in the market under Barra's leadership, with a clear strategic direction toward future mobility solutions like EVs and autonomous vehicles.

Mary Barra's leadership at General Motors is a striking example of effective leadership in a complex and rapidly evolving industry. Her ability to navigate the company through crises, her forward-thinking commitment to innovation and sustainability, and her embodiment of Servant and Conscious Leadership principles have not only steered GM through challenging times but have also positioned the company for future success. Barra's tenure highlights the importance of adaptive, empathetic, and responsible leadership in the modern corporate world.

These case studies can highlight the strengths and limitations of each approach and demonstrate how the integration of Servant and Conscious Leadership practices can lead to more effective, ethical, and sustainable leadership.

FUTURE DIRECTIONS FOR SERVANT AND CONSCIOUS LEADERSHIP MODELS

Looking to the future, both Servant and Conscious Leadership models are well-positioned to address the challenges of the modern world. As organizations become more aware of the importance of ethical leadership and the impact of their actions on society and the environment, these leadership styles are likely to gain more prominence.

The future of these models may involve a greater emphasis on sustainability, social responsibility, and global awareness. Leaders will need to adapt to a rapidly changing world, where technological advancements, environmental concerns, and social dynamics require a more flexible, aware, and compassionate leadership approach.

While Servant and Conscious Leadership have distinct foundations and approaches, their integration can lead to a more comprehensive, effective, and ethical leadership style. As we look to the future, the principles of both models will be crucial in guiding leaders through the complexities of the modern world.

CHAPTER 7 EXERCISES: CULTIVATING SERVANT LEADERSHIP IN PRACTICE

The following exercises focus on Servant Leadership, ensuring practical, individual application. These will help you integrate the principles of empowering others, fostering inclusivity, and leading with humility and service into your leadership approach.

Exercise 1: The Leadership Reflection Journal

Objective: To deepen self-awareness about how your leadership style aligns with the principles of Servant Leadership.
  Instructions:

- **Define Your Leadership Approach:**
  - Take 10 minutes to write down how you currently lead. Consider:
  - How do you prioritize the needs of your team? How do you empower others?
  - Where do you struggle with letting go of control?
- **Assess Servant Leadership Alignment:**
  - Review your responses and compare them to the key Servant Leadership traits: empathy, stewardship, humility, and a commitment to others' growth.
- **Identify an Area for Growth:**
  - Choose one aspect of Servant Leadership you'd like to develop (e.g., listening more actively, delegating more trustingly, or prioritizing team well-being).

- **Set an Intention:**
  - Over the next week, apply this principle consciously and write a short reflection on how it impacted your leadership interactions.

Exercise 2: The Empowerment Challenge

Objective: To shift from a directive leadership style to an empowering one by fostering autonomy and trust.

   Instructions:

- **Identify an Opportunity to Empower Someone:**
  - Choose a task or decision you usually take full ownership of but could delegate or share responsibility for.
- **Select a Team Member to Entrust:**
  - Consider who would benefit from the experience, ensuring they have the support and resources needed.
- **Communicate Trust and Clear Expectations:**
  - When delegating, use language that expresses confidence in their ability (e.g., "I know you can handle this" rather than "I need you to do this"). Be clear about the desired outcome but allow flexibility in the approach.
- **Observe and Reflect:**
  - **After the task is completed, reflect on:**
    Did the person take ownership?
  - What impact did this have on their confidence and development? How did it affect your role as a leader?
- **Commit to Delegating More Often:**
  - Identify additional areas where you can empower your team rather than control tasks.

Exercise 3: The Servant Leadership Listening Test

Objective: To strengthen active listening and empathy—two fundamental traits of Servant Leadership.

   Instructions:

- **Engage in a One-on-One Conversation:**
  - Choose a conversation (work or personal) where you will practice deep, undistracted listening.

- **Apply Servant Leadership Listening Techniques:**
  - Avoid interrupting or formulating responses while the other person speaks. Use open-ended follow-up questions ("Tell me more about that…").
  - Paraphrase and summarize their points to show you understand.
    Reflect on Your Listening Skills:
    After the conversation, ask yourself: Did I truly listen or was I waiting for my turn to speak?
  - Did the other person feel heard and valued?
  - How can I improve my listening to foster a more inclusive and service-oriented leadership style?

Exercise 4: The Servant Leader's Decision-Making Test

Objective: To make leadership decisions through the lens of Servant Leadership, prioritizing the well-being of your team and organization.
  Instructions:

- Think About a Recent Decision You Made as a Leader.
  - Who was impacted by this decision?
  - Did it serve the long-term growth and well-being of those involved? Did you gather input from others, or was it made in isolation?
- Reframe the Decision from a Servant Leadership Perspective:
  - Would the decision have changed if the team's development and well-being were the primary factors?
  - If the decision focused only on short-term efficiency, what long-term consequences might arise?
- Commit to Making Future Decisions with a Servant Leadership Approach: The next time you face a leadership decision, consult your team first.
  - **Ask:** How does this serve those I lead?
  - Prioritize long-term team growth over short-term convenience.

Exercise 5: The Gratitude Leadership Habit

Objective: To cultivate a leadership style that recognizes and appreciates the contributions of others.
  Instructions:

- **Observe Contributions:**
  - Throughout the day, pay attention to the small and large ways your team members contribute to success.

- **Express Meaningful Gratitude:**
  1. Take five minutes daily to express genuine appreciation to a team member.
  2. Be specific—instead of "Great job," say "Your attention to detail in today's report helped us avoid a major issue—thank you."
  3. Deliver praise verbally or in writing, ensuring authenticity. Reflect on the Impact:
  4. How did the person react?
  5. How did expressing gratitude make you feel?
  6. How does this practice contribute to a Servant Leadership culture?
  7. Make Gratitude a Habit: Commit to regularly acknowledging the contributions of others as an integral part of your leadership approach.

8

Fostering a Conscious Organizational Culture

Customers will never love a company until the employees love it first.

– Simon Sinek

A conscious culture is an organizational ethos characterized by mindfulness, ethical values, and a deep awareness of the organization's impact on all stakeholders, including employees, customers, the community, and the environment. It's a culture where every action and decision is made with a deliberate consideration of its broader implications, both within and outside the organization.

In a conscious culture, the focus extends beyond profitability and productivity to encompass the well-being and development of its people, and a commitment to social and environmental responsibility. This culture is underpinned by principles such as transparency, empathy, inclusivity, and sustainability. It encourages continuous learning, open communication, and a shared sense of purpose among all members.

Such a culture is not static but dynamic, evolving with the changing needs of its stakeholders and the global landscape. It fosters an environment where employees feel genuinely connected to the organization's mission, are engaged in their work, and are empowered to contribute their best.

In essence, a conscious culture represents a holistic approach to organizational life, one that values and integrates the human aspect of business with ethical practices and mindful leadership.

DOI: 10.1201/9781003488705-8

THE BUILDING BLOCKS OF A CONSCIOUS CULTURE

Creating a conscious organizational culture is akin to crafting a masterpiece; it requires vision, dedication, and a deep understanding of the various elements that make up the whole. The building blocks of such a culture are multifaceted, each contributing to an environment where employees feel valued, engaged, and aligned with the organization's core values and objectives.

The first building block is a clear and compelling vision. This vision should resonate with employees on a personal level, transcending mere corporate goals to encompass broader social and environmental responsibilities. It's about creating a narrative that employees can connect with, one that gives meaning and purpose to their work.

Next is the establishment of core values. These values should be more than words on a page; they should be lived experiences, embedded in every aspect of the organization's operations. From decision-making processes to everyday interactions, these values should serve as a compass, guiding behavior and fostering a sense of shared purpose.

Another crucial element is open and transparent communication. This means not just sharing information but also encouraging dialogue, feedback, and the free exchange of ideas. It's about creating channels where employees feel heard and where their input is valued and acted upon.

Finally, a conscious culture is underpinned by a commitment to continuous learning and development. This involves not just professional growth but also personal development, encouraging employees to explore their potential and contribute their unique skills and perspectives to the organization.

THE LEADER'S ROLE IN SHAPING CULTURE

In the intricate journey of building a conscious organizational culture, the role of the leader emerges as both pivotal and profound. Leaders are not merely at the helm of decision-making; they are the architects and sculptors of the workplace culture. Their influence extends far beyond strategy and operations, deeply embedding into the very ethos and norms that define the organizational environment. This section explores the multifaceted role of leaders in shaping and nurturing a conscious culture within their organizations.

Leaders in a conscious culture transcend the traditional boundaries of decision-making. They are visionaries who paint a picture of what the organization can aspire to be. Their role is akin to that of a coach or a mentor, guiding and inspiring their teams toward a shared vision. The most impactful leaders understand that their actions and behaviors send powerful signals that reverberate across the organization. They lead not just with words but through example, embodying the values and principles that they wish to see reflected in their organization.

Consider a leader who advocates for work-life balance. If they consistently work late into the night, sending emails at all hours, the message to the team contradicts the stated value.

Conversely, a leader who respects boundaries and encourages their team to do the same reinforces a culture of balance and respect.

A critical aspect of a leader's role in shaping culture is fostering an environment of trust and psychological safety. This concept goes beyond the traditional notion of a safe workplace; it's about creating a space where employees feel empowered to take risks, voice their opinions, and embrace their vulnerabilities without fear of retribution or ridicule. It's about leaders showing their own vulnerability, openly admitting when they don't have all the answers, and encouraging their team to share in the journey of learning and discovery.

For instance, when a leader openly discusses a project that didn't go as planned and encourages the team to share insights and learnings, it sets a tone of openness and continuous improvement. This approach not only enhances learning but also builds a foundation of trust where employees feel valued and heard.

Another vital role of leaders in conscious cultures is bridging the gap between day-to-day activities and the larger organizational vision and values. It's about making the vision tangible and relevant to every team member. Leaders must articulate not just what the organization aims to achieve but also why these goals matter. They need to help employees connect their individual roles and contributions to the broader objectives and values of the organization.

Imagine a company that values sustainability. A leader in this organization would not only implement sustainable practices but also help employees understand how their work contributes to this value. This might involve sharing stories of how the company's products or services positively impact the environment or highlighting individual contributions to sustainability initiatives.

The journey to nurturing a conscious culture is continuous and evolving. Leaders must remain committed to personal growth and development, as their evolution directly impacts the culture they are trying to cultivate. They need to stay attuned to the changing dynamics within their teams and the external environment, adapting their leadership style and strategies to meet these evolving needs.

For example, as the workforce becomes more diverse, leaders must adapt by fostering an inclusive culture that respects and celebrates diversity. This might involve training programs, inclusive policies, and practices, and an open dialogue about diversity and inclusion within the organization.

The leader's role in shaping a conscious organizational culture is multifaceted and dynamic. It requires a blend of visionary leadership, role modeling, fostering trust and psychological safety, and connecting the day-to-day work with the larger organizational vision and values. Leaders in conscious cultures are more than decision-makers; they are the catalysts for a culture that values growth, learning, and the well-being of all its members. By embracing these roles, leaders can create a workplace environment that is not only productive and successful but also nurturing and fulfilling for everyone involved (Figure 8.1).

STRATEGIES FOR CULTURAL TRANSFORMATION

Transforming an organizational culture is akin to steering a large ship through uncharted waters. It's a journey that demands not only skill and

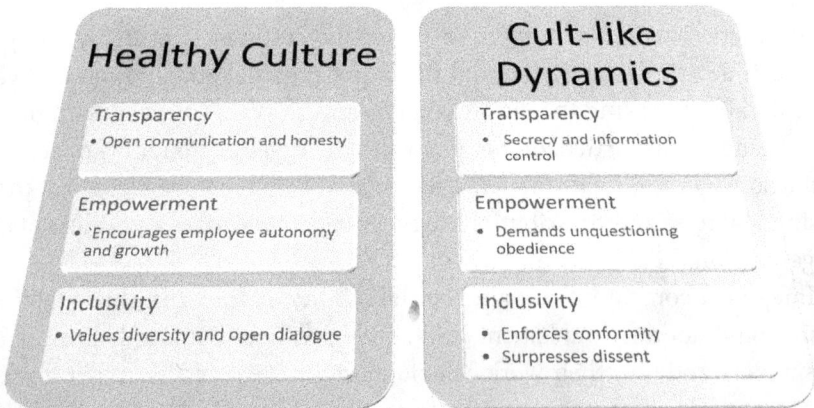

Healthy Culture

Transparency
- Open communication and honesty

Empowerment
- Encourages employee autonomy and growth

Inclusivity
- Values diversity and open dialogue

Cult-like Dynamics

Transparency
- Secrecy and information control

Empowerment
- Demands unquestioning obedience

Inclusivity
- Enforces conformity
- Surpresses dissent

FIGURE 8.1
Healthy Culture vs. Cult-Like Dynamics.

precision but also a deep understanding of the currents and winds that influence its path. This transformation is no small feat; it requires a strategic approach, one that is thoughtful, intentional, and aligned with the organization's goals and values. In the context of Conscious Leadership, this transformation becomes even more nuanced, as it involves cultivating a culture that is not only effective and efficient but also mindful, ethical, and attuned to the broader impact on society and the environment.

The first step in this transformative journey is to gain a deep understanding of the existing culture. This involves peeling back the layers to uncover the underlying beliefs, behaviors, and practices that define the current state. It's like an archaeologist uncovering the layers of an ancient city, each layer offering insights into the values and norms that have been built up over time. This understanding is crucial, as it provides the foundation upon which the new culture will be built. Leaders must engage in active listening, open dialogue, and perhaps even utilize surveys and focus groups to gather a comprehensive view of the current cultural landscape.

Once the current culture is understood, the next step is to envision the desired future state. This vision should be compelling and inspiring, painting a picture of what the organization can aspire to become. It should align with the organization's goals and values, providing a north star that guides the transformation. This visioning process is not just a top-down exercise; it involves engaging with employees at all levels, inviting them to co-create a shared vision of the future. It's a process that fosters buy-in and enthusiasm, as people are more likely to support a culture they have helped shape.

The implementation of this cultural transformation is where the real work begins. It involves aligning policies, processes, and systems with the desired culture. This might mean revising performance metrics to include measures of collaboration and innovation, redesigning training programs to focus on Conscious Leadership skills, or rethinking reward systems to align with new values. It's a comprehensive approach that touches every aspect of the organization.

One of the most critical elements of this transformation is communication. Leaders must communicate the vision and the steps being taken to achieve it clearly and consistently. This communication should be ongoing, not a one-time announcement. It should be a dialogue, not a monologue, inviting feedback and discussion. This open communication helps to keep the momentum going, ensuring that the cultural transformation remains a top priority.

Another key aspect of this journey is the role of leaders as role models. Leaders must embody the new culture in their actions and behaviors. They must walk the talk, demonstrating the values and practices that define the new culture. This role modeling is powerful, as employees often look to their leaders for cues on how to behave. When leaders consistently demonstrate the new culture, it sends a strong message that this is not just a passing fad but a new way of being.

Measuring progress is also vital. Cultural transformation is a complex process, and it can be challenging to gauge success. However, setting clear metrics and regularly assessing progress is essential. This might involve regular surveys to gauge employee engagement and satisfaction, tracking progress against specific cultural goals, or assessing changes in key behaviors and practices. This measurement not only provides a sense of how far the organization has come but also identifies areas where further work is needed.

Finally, it's important to celebrate successes along the way. Cultural transformation is a long and often challenging journey. Celebrating milestones, no matter how small, helps to maintain enthusiasm and commitment. It's a way of acknowledging the hard work and progress that has been made, reinforcing the belief that the desired culture is achievable.

The transformation of an organizational culture is a significant undertaking, one that requires a strategic, thoughtful, and intentional approach. It involves understanding the current culture, envisioning a new future, aligning policies and practices, communicating effectively, role modeling, measuring progress, and celebrating successes. In the context of Conscious Leadership, this transformation takes on an added dimension, as it involves cultivating a culture that is not only effective but also mindful, ethical, and socially responsible. It's a journey that requires patience, persistence, and a deep commitment to creating an organization that not only succeeds in the marketplace but also contributes positively to society and the planet.

MEASURING CULTURAL ALIGNMENT AND CONSCIOUSNESS

Measuring the alignment and consciousness of an organizational culture is crucial in understanding its effectiveness and impact. This measurement is not just about quantitative metrics but also qualitative insights.

Leadership Reflection

Do we promote open and honest communication?

Are employees encouraged to provide feedback without fear?

How do we recognize and celebrate diversity within our team?

What measures are in place to support employee well-being?

Are our organizational values clearlky defined and practicl?

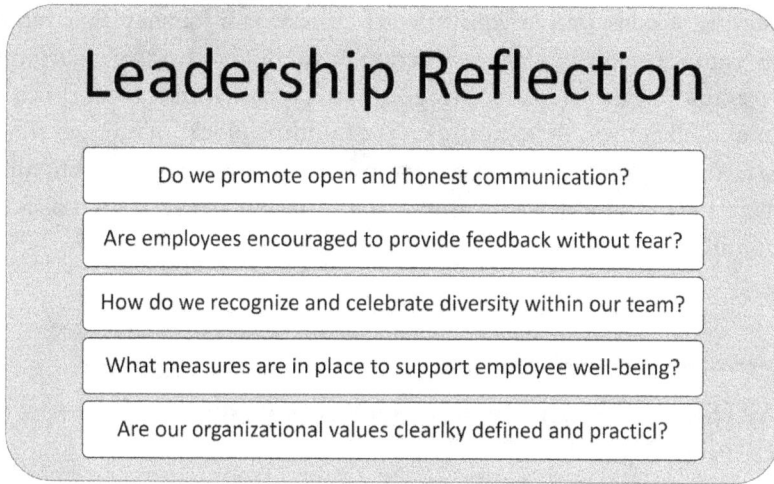

FIGURE 8.2
The Leadership Reflection Checklist.

Surveys and questionnaires can be used to gauge employee perceptions of the culture, their level of engagement, and their alignment with the organization's values. Employee feedback and exit interviews can also provide valuable insights into the health of the culture.

Another important aspect of measurement is the assessment of leadership behaviors. This involves evaluating whether leaders are modeling the values and practices that define the desired culture (Figure 8.2).

SUSTAINABLE PRACTICES IN CONSCIOUS CULTURES

Sustainability in a conscious culture goes beyond environmental practices; it encompasses the long-term health and viability of the organization. This involves creating practices that are not only good for the business but also for the employees, the community, and the environment.

One key aspect of sustainability is the focus on employee well-being. This means not just physical well-being but also mental and emotional health. It involves creating policies and practices that support work-life balance, encourage healthy lifestyles, and provide support for mental health.

Another aspect is the commitment to social and environmental responsibility. This involves integrating sustainable practices into every aspect of the organization's operations, from resource use to supply chain management.

Fostering a conscious organizational culture is a journey that requires vision, commitment, and strategic action. It's about creating an environment where employees feel valued, engaged, and aligned with the organization's values and objectives. By focusing on the building blocks of culture, the role of the leader, strategies for transformation, measurement, and sustainability, organizations can cultivate a culture that is not only effective but also conscious and aligned with the broader good.

CHAPTER 8 EXERCISES: BUILDING A CONSCIOUS ORGANIZATIONAL CULTURE

These exercises focus on fostering a conscious, ethical, and inclusive workplace culture. Each exercise provides practical, individual applications to help leaders cultivate trust, shared values, and psychological safety in their organizations.

Exercise 1: Culture Audit—Identifying Strengths and Gaps

- **Observe Your Workplace Culture:**
  Over the next few days, pay close attention to **how people interact, communicate, and engage** in the organization.
  - Are employees comfortable sharing ideas and concerns? Do teams collaborate, or do silos exist?
  - Is leadership transparent about decisions? How are mistakes handled—blame or learning?
- **Document Your Observations:**
  - Write down examples of **healthy cultural behaviors** and **areas that feel misaligned** with a Conscious Leadership approach.
- **Identify One Area for Growth:**
  - Choose **one cultural element** (e.g., openness to feedback, trust, inclusion, recognition) where improvement is needed.
- **Commit to a Leadership Action:**
  - Decide on **one Conscious Leadership behavior** you will adopt to strengthen this aspect of culture. Examples:
- Encourage open dialogue by **asking for team feedback** in your next meeting.
- Model transparency by **sharing decision-making processes** more openly. Build trust by **giving team members autonomy** over a project.

- **Reflect on the Impact:**
  After implementing this change, assess: How did people respond?
  - Did engagement or collaboration improve?
  - What adjustments are needed for long-term impact?

Exercise 2: Aligning Leadership Actions with Core Values

Objective: To evaluate whether your daily leadership actions align with your organization's values.
  Instructions:

- **Write Down Your Organization's Core Values:**
  If they are not clearly defined, list the values **you believe should guide decision-making** (e.g., integrity, innovation, inclusivity).
- **Analyze Your Leadership Actions:**
  Over the next week, assess whether your decisions, meetings, and communications reflect these values.
  - Are policies aligned with stated values?
  - Are hiring and promotion practices **fair and inclusive**? Does leadership model ethical decision-making?
- **Identify Gaps:**
  If any of your behaviors or company practices **do not align** with the values, note them.
- **Choose One Area for Immediate Action:**
  Commit to **adjusting one habit or policy** to better reflect the organization's values. Examples:
  - If **innovation** is a core value, **allow employees more creative freedom** in projects.
  - If **transparency** is a value, **share more context behind leadership decisions**.
  - If **collaboration** is a value, **break down silos between departments**.
- **Review and Adjust:**
  Reflect after one month—has the small change influenced the workplace positively? What next step can further reinforce alignment?

Exercise 3: Creating Psychological Safety in Your Team

Objective: To cultivate an environment where employees feel safe expressing ideas, concerns, and challenges.

Instructions:

- **Assess Current Psychological Safety:**
  - Do team members hesitate to speak up in meetings?
  - Are mistakes openly discussed, or do people fear blame?
  - Do employees feel comfortable challenging leadership decisions?
- **Encourage Safe Conversations:**
  - In your next meeting, **express openness to new ideas and diverse opinions.**
- **Acknowledge past mistakes and model vulnerability.**
  - Use **inclusive language** like "What do you think?" and "I appreciate your perspective."
- **Create a Feedback Loop:**
  - **Privately ask team members: "What would help you feel more comfortable sharing your thoughts?"**
  - Implement small changes based on responses (e.g., anonymous feedback channels, designated brainstorming time in meetings).
- **Monitor and Adjust:**
  Over time, observe whether people become **more engaged and willing to contribute**. Adjust your approach as needed.

Exercise 4: Leading by Example—The Leadership Behavior Test

Objective: To examine whether your leadership behaviors reflect the culture you want to create.
  Instructions:

- **Describe the Ideal Culture You Want to Build:**
  - What values should be at the core?
  - How should people interact, collaborate, and solve problems? How should leadership communicate and make decisions?
- **Compare Your Daily Actions:**
  Over the next week, reflect on your own behaviors and ask:
  - Do I listen actively and engage with my team? Am I transparent in my decision-making?
  - Do I model the values I expect from others?
- **Seek Feedback:**
  Ask a trusted colleague or direct report:

"What is one way I could better model our values?"
- **Commit to a Leadership Adjustment:**
  Choose one small habit change that aligns your actions with your cultural vision.

Exercise 5: Redefining Success in a Conscious Culture

Objective: To shift from a traditional success mindset (profits, efficiency) to a **balanced, people-focused** approach.
  Instructions:
  List Your Current Success Metrics:
  How do you currently define success in your role?

- Are these metrics **only financial and performance-driven**, or do they include **employee well-being, growth, and collaboration?**
- Expand Your Definition of Success:

What **non-financial indicators** should be part of a conscious culture? Examples:

- Team engagement and retention. Employee happiness and motivation.

Innovation and adaptability.

- **Track One New Cultural Success Metric:**
  Choose **one measure** (e.g., employee engagement, trust level, inclusivity) and actively track it for a month.
- **Adjust Leadership Strategies:**
  Based on what you observe, modify your approach to **balance traditional business goals with cultural well-being**.

Engage in relevant courses, workshops, or mentorship programs.

9

Common Pitfalls for Conscious Leaders

In the exploration of Conscious Leadership, it's essential to begin by understanding the common pitfalls that leaders might encounter. Leadership, much like a journey through uncharted territories, is fraught with challenges that can test the resolve, values, and adaptability of any leader.

One such pitfall is the illusion of infallibility. Leaders, conscious of their role or not, often fall prey to the belief that their decisions are beyond reproach. This misstep, subtly woven into the fabric of leadership, can lead to a disconnect with the team and a blind spot in decision-making processes. As John C. Maxwell aptly stated, "A leader is one who knows the way, goes the way, and shows the way." This knowing, going, and showing must be grounded in humility and the acceptance that mistakes are inevitable and essential for growth.

Another common pitfall is the lack of self-awareness. Conscious Leadership is deeply rooted in understanding one's emotions, motivations, and the impact one has on others. Without this introspection, a leader may unintentionally steer their team toward disengagement or misunderstanding. To quote Socrates, "Know thyself," a simple yet profound counsel that holds true for leaders striving to be conscious and effective.

Leaders may also encounter the trap of overcommitment. In their zeal to make a difference, they stretch themselves too thin, leading to burnout and reduced effectiveness. As Ralph Waldo Emerson once said, "Moderation in all things, especially moderation." Leaders must find balance, prioritizing tasks and delegating when necessary to maintain their efficacy and well-being (Figure 9.1).

DOI: 10.1201/9781003488705-9

FIGURE 9.1
Five Key Toxic Leadership Traits.

STRATEGIES FOR RESILIENCE AND ADAPTABILITY

The heart of Conscious Leadership lies in resilience and adaptability—key traits that allow leaders to navigate the ever-changing landscapes of their professional and personal lives. To cultivate resilience, leaders must develop a mindset that views challenges as opportunities for growth. This perspective aligns with the words of Helen Keller, who said, "Character cannot be developed in ease and quiet. Only through experience of trial and suffering can the soul be strengthened, ambition inspired, and success achieved."

Adaptability, however, calls for a leader to be fluid in their approach, adjusting their strategies and tactics as circumstances evolve. It is akin to what Charles Darwin observed, "It is not the strongest of the species that survive, nor the most intelligent, but the one most responsive to change." In leadership, this means being open to new ideas, feedback, and the willingness to pivot when necessary.

One effective strategy for fostering resilience and adaptability is to cultivate a growth mindset. This concept, championed by Carol Dweck, emphasizes the belief that abilities and intelligence can be developed. Leaders with a growth mindset are more likely to embrace challenges, persist in the face of setbacks, learn from criticism, and find lessons and inspiration in the success of others.

Another strategy is to practice mindfulness and emotional intelligence. Mindfulness helps leaders stay grounded in the present moment, reducing stress and enhancing decision-making capabilities. Emotional intelligence, comprising self-awareness, self-regulation, motivation, empathy, and social skills, equips leaders to manage their emotions and understand those of others, fostering a harmonious and productive work environment (Figure 9.2).

Case Studies: When Conscious Leadership is Tested

Delving deeper into the realm of Conscious Leadership, we turn our attention to real-world scenarios where these principles are put to the test. These case studies serve as practical illustrations, shedding light on the application of Conscious Leadership in challenging situations.

One such case is that of a tech startup facing a significant market downturn. The CEO, known for her visionary approach and strong ethical standards, found herself at a crossroads. Revenue was plummeting, and investor pressure was mounting. In this crucible, her commitment to Conscious Leadership was tested. Instead of resorting to mass layoffs or unethical practices to inflate short-term results, she chose to transparently communicate

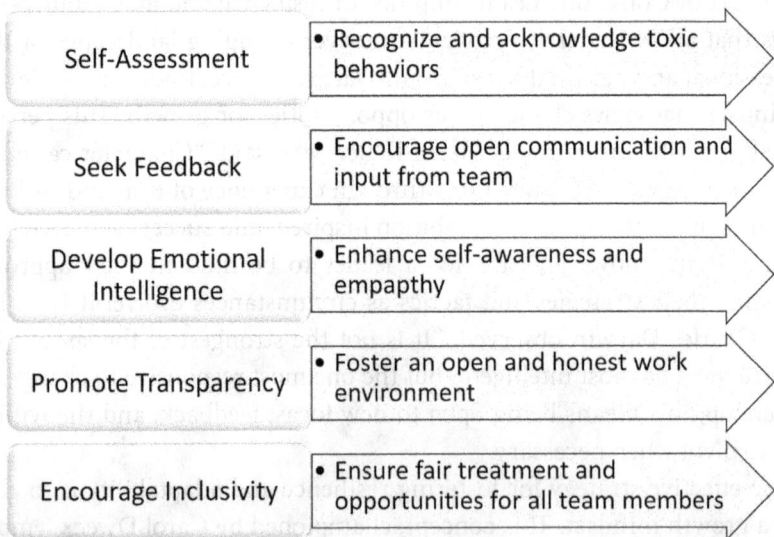

Self-Assessment	• Recognize and acknowledge toxic behaviors
Seek Feedback	• Encourage open communication and input from team
Develop Emotional Intelligence	• Enhance self-awareness and empapthy
Promote Transparency	• Foster an open and honest work environment
Encourage Inclusivity	• Ensure fair treatment and opportunities for all team members

FIGURE 9.2
Steps to Correct Toxic Leadership.

the challenges with her team and re-strategize with a focus on long-term sustainability and core values. Her decision echoed the sentiment of Winston Churchill, who once said, "Success is not final, failure is not fatal: It is the courage to continue that counts." This CEO's courage to uphold her values in the face of adversity not only steered the company through tough times but also reinforced the team's trust and commitment.

Another instance involves a non-profit organization grappling with internal conflict and misalignment of goals. The leader, a staunch advocate for participative management, utilized this challenge as an opportunity to realign the organization's mission with the team's values and aspirations. He facilitated open discussions, encouraging team members to voice their concerns and ideas. This approach is reminiscent of the wisdom in Lao Tzu's words, "A leader is best when people barely know he exists, when his work is done, his aim fulfilled, they will say: we did it ourselves." By empowering his team, the leader not only resolved the conflict but also fostered a stronger, more cohesive organizational culture.

STAYING THE COURSE: MAINTAINING CONSCIOUS LEADERSHIP PRINCIPLES UNDER PRESSURE

The true test of Conscious Leadership often occurs under pressure—when the stakes are high, and the temptation to veer off the ethical path is strongest. Staying the course in such times demands a deep-rooted commitment to one's values and principles.

One crucial aspect of maintaining Conscious Leadership under pressure is having a clear vision and purpose. This vision serves as a guiding star, keeping leaders aligned with their goals and values even when faced with challenging circumstances. As Viktor E. Frankl, author of 'Man's Search for Meaning', profoundly stated, "Those who have a 'why' to live, can bear with almost any 'how'." A leader's strong sense of purpose enables them to navigate through tough times with resilience and integrity.

Another important aspect is the cultivation of self-discipline and consistency. These qualities ensure that a leader's actions and decisions remain aligned with their principles, regardless of external pressures or temptations. As Aristotle put it, "We are what we repeatedly do. Excellence, then, is not an act, but a habit." For conscious leaders, this habit of excellence is underpinned by their unwavering adherence to their core values and ethical standards.

THE ROLE OF SUPPORT SYSTEMS IN OVERCOMING LEADERSHIP OBSTACLES

The journey of Conscious Leadership is not one to be embarked upon alone. The support of mentors, peers, and team members plays a vital role in helping leaders overcome obstacles and stay true to their principles.

Mentors, with their wealth of experience and wisdom, provide invaluable guidance and perspective, helping leaders navigate complex situations. As Isaac Newton famously said, "If I have seen further it is by standing on the shoulders of Giants." The mentor-mentee relationship in leadership acts as a beacon, illuminating paths through the mentor's insights and experiences.

Equally important is the support of peers and team members. A culture of mutual support, open communication, and collective problem-solving creates a resilient and adaptive environment.

This collaborative approach is summed up in the African proverb, "If you want to go fast, go alone. If you want to go far, go together." In Conscious Leadership, going far means building a legacy of positive impact and sustainable success, achieved through the collective efforts and support of the entire team.

INTEGRATING CONSCIOUS LEADERSHIP INTO EVERYDAY PRACTICES

The essence of Conscious Leadership transcends theoretical understanding and finds its true value in daily integration. It's about transforming insights into actions, principles into practices. This integration is the bridge between knowing and doing, between aspiring and becoming a conscious leader.

One pivotal practice is continuous self-reflection. Conscious leaders regularly take time to introspect, examining their decisions, actions, and their impact on others. This practice aligns with the wisdom of Socrates, who emphasized the importance of self-examination with his famous maxim, "The unexamined life is not worth living." Through self-reflection, leaders gain deeper insights into their strengths and areas for improvement, fostering personal growth and effective leadership.

Another practice is active listening. Conscious leaders understand that effective communication is not just about conveying one's ideas but also about truly understanding others' perspectives. As Stephen R. Covey, author of "The 7 Habits of Highly Effective People," eloquently put it, "Most people do not listen with the intent to understand; they listen with the intent to reply." Active listening fosters trust, respect, and collaboration, creating a strong foundation for team cohesion and effective leadership.

Developing emotional intelligence is also crucial. This involves not only being aware of and managing one's own emotions but also recognizing and influencing the emotions of others. Daniel Goleman, a pioneer in emotional intelligence research, highlighted its significance in leadership, noting that emotional intelligence accounts for nearly 90% of what sets high performers apart from peers with similar technical skills and knowledge.

Lastly, Conscious leaders are committed to lifelong learning. They recognize that leadership is a journey, not a destination. As Mahatma Gandhi said, "Live as if you were to die tomorrow. Learn as if you were to live forever." This mindset drives leaders to continually seek new knowledge, skills, and experiences, ensuring they remain effective and relevant in an ever-changing world.

Conscious Leadership is a journey marked by continuous growth, ethical decision-making, and a deep commitment to positively impacting those around us. It's about leading with purpose, empathy, and resilience, staying true to one's values even in the face of adversity.

As we reflect on the various aspects of Conscious Leadership discussed in this chapter, let us remember the profound words of Nelson Mandela, a paragon of leadership and resilience: "The greatest glory in living lies not in never falling, but in rising every time we fall." This sentiment encapsulates the essence of Conscious Leadership—rising above challenges, learning from experiences, and persistently striving to be a better leader for the greater good.

CHAPTER 9 EXERCISES: OVERCOMING COMMON LEADERSHIP PITFALLS

These exercises focus on identifying and correcting unconscious leadership habits that can undermine team trust, engagement, and effectiveness. They will help you strengthen self-awareness, improve leadership behaviors, and foster a Conscious Leadership approach.

Exercise 1: Leadership Pitfall Self-assessment

Objective: To identify unconscious leadership behaviors that may be limiting team performance.

Instructions:
Identify Leadership Habits:
Reflect on the past month and consider moments where you:

- Micromanaged rather than trusted your team.
- Reacted emotionally instead of responding with intention. Resisted feedback or dismissed an idea too quickly.
- Prioritized short-term results over long-term growth.
- **Rate Yourself:**
  Use the scale 1-5 where 1 Rarely) and 5Often) to assess how frequently these behaviors occur.

Identify Your Top Pitfall:
Choose one leadership behavior that most needs improvement.

- **Set a Correction Plan:**
  - Write one specific action you will take over the next two weeks to address this pitfall. Examples:
  - If you tend to micromanage, commit to delegating a project without interference. If you often dismiss feedback, create an open-feedback session where you only listen and reflect.
- **Track Progress:**
  After two weeks, evaluate whether your change positively impacted your leadership effectiveness.

Exercise 2: The Trust Rebuilding Challenge

Objective: To repair trust if it has been weakened by unconscious leadership mistakes.
  Instructions:

- **Identify a Trust Gap:**
  - Reflect on a recent situation where trust may have been compromised (e.g., broken commitments, inconsistent messaging, or lack of transparency).
- **Acknowledge the Impact:**
  - Write down how this action (or inaction) may have affected your team or an individual. Consider:
  - How did this behavior impact morale or motivation?
  - Did it create uncertainty or hesitation in decision-making? Has communication been affected?

- **Plan a Trust-Building Action:**
  - Choose one intentional action to rebuild trust:
  - If you failed to follow through on a commitment, address it directly and set clearer expectations.
  - If you lacked transparency, provide more context in future communications. If you neglected recognition, make it a priority to acknowledge contributions.
- **Implement and Observe:**
  - Carry out the trust-rebuilding action and monitor how the person or team responds.

Exercise 3: Mastering Constructive Feedback

Objective: To shift from criticism-based leadership to growth-oriented feedback.
  Instructions:

- **Recall a Recent Feedback Moment:**
  1. Think of a time you gave feedback—was it clear, supportive, and constructive?
- **Rewrite the Feedback Using the SBI Model:**
  1. Situation: Describe the context neutrally (e.g., "In yesterday's meeting…"). Behavior: State what was observed without judgment (e.g., "I noticed you interrupted others several times…")
  2. Impact: Explain the effect of the behavior (e.g., "This made it harder for the team to discuss ideas openly.")
  3. Improvement Suggestion: Offer a positive, forward-thinking suggestion (e.g., "Next time, let's focus on creating space for everyone to contribute.")
- **Apply in Real-Time:**
  1. Use this structure for your next feedback conversation and observe how it improves receptivity.

Exercise 4: Breaking the Reactivity Cycle

Objective: To move from emotionally reactive leadership to intentional, mindful responses.
  Instructions:

- **Identify a Trigger:**
  - Think of a situation where you often react impulsively—such as receiving criticism, handling mistakes, or being challenged.

- **Pause and Reflect:**
  - The next time this occurs:
  - Pause for 10 seconds before responding.
  - Name the emotion you feel (frustration, defensiveness, etc.). Ask yourself: "What response aligns with my leadership values?"
- **Respond with Intention:**
  - Instead of reacting immediately, take a breath and respond with clarity and purpose.
- **Evaluate the Outcome:**
  - Did your response improve the conversation? What would you adjust next time?

Exercise 5: The Delegation Confidence Builder

Objective: To overcome micromanagement and strengthen trust in your team.
  Instructions:

- **Choose a Task to Delegate:**
  - Identify a responsibility you tend to control but could entrust to a team member.
- **Select the Right Person:**
  - Pick someone capable and willing to take on the task. Clearly Define the Outcome: Instead of detailing every step, describe the desired result and let them determine the approach.
- **Resist Micromanaging:**
  - Do not interfere unless truly necessary. Instead, schedule a check-in to discuss progress.
- **Assess the Impact:**
  - Reflect on how delegation improved efficiency and team empowerment.

Exercise 5: Continuous Learning

Objective: To commit to ongoing personal and professional development.
  Instructions:

- **Identify Growth Areas:**
  - Determine skills or knowledge you wish to enhance.
- **Set Learning Goals:**
  - Establish specific, measurable objectives for your development.
- **Pursue Development Opportunities:**
  - Engage in relevant courses, workshops, or mentorship programs.

10

Measuring the Impact of Conscious Leadership

In the realm of Conscious Leadership, success is not merely a measure of financial gain or rank attainment; it is an intricate tapestry woven from the threads of ethical decisions, community impact, and sustainable practices. This nuanced approach stands in stark contrast to the more traditional metrics of leadership success, which often prioritize tangible achievements and immediate results. John C. Maxwell, a seminal figure in leadership thought, often highlighted the importance of values and influence in leadership. He eloquently stated, "A leader is one who knows the way, goes the way, and shows the way." This sentiment captures the essence of Conscious Leadership—it is about setting a path not only for oneself but also for the greater good of all.

In the journey of a conscious leader, success is not a destination but a continuous process of growth, learning, and ethical decision-making. It's akin to planting a tree; the true impact is not seen in the immediate sprouting of the sapling but in the eventual growth of a sturdy, life-giving tree. This metaphor aligns with Maxwell's emphasis on long-term vision and influence in leadership. As he once said, "Leadership is not about titles, positions, or flowcharts. It is about one life influencing another." This influence is most profoundly felt not in boardrooms or flashy accolades but in the quiet transformation of a leader's immediate community and, by extension, the world.

Conscious leaders measure their success by the depth and breadth of their impact. They seek to foster environments where creativity, ethical practices, and communal well-being flourish. This is a departure from a purely profit-driven or hierarchical view of success, akin to Maxwell's teaching on the value of Servant Leadership. He opined, "People don't care how much you know until they know how much you care." Thus, the success of a

DOI: 10.1201/9781003488705-10

conscious leader is intricately linked to their ability to empathize, connect, and nurture growth in others—a far cry from the traditional corporate ladder-climbing.

However, Conscious Leadership also recognizes the reality of business and organizational needs. Success in this context is not an abandonment of profitability or efficiency but their redefinition through a lens of sustainability and ethical responsibility. This balance between pragmatism and idealism is a hallmark of Maxwell's teachings. He recognized that effective leadership involves navigating the practicalities of the present while being guided by the moral compass of long-term vision and integrity.

Conscious Leadership redefines success by prioritizing ethical decision-making, community impact, and sustainable growth. This approach aligns with Maxwell's insights on the transformative power of leadership grounded in values and influence. It's a journey that transcends traditional metrics, seeking a harmonious balance between business acumen and moral responsibility.

TOOLS AND METRICS FOR ASSESSING LEADERSHIP IMPACT

In the pursuit of assessing the impact of Conscious Leadership, a blend of both qualitative and quantitative tools is essential. Metrics such as employee engagement scores, customer satisfaction rates, and financial performance are traditional yet crucial indicators. However, in the realm of Conscious Leadership, these are complemented by more nuanced measures. For instance, evaluating the ethical implications of business decisions, the level of community engagement, and the sustainability of practices are equally vital. This dual approach aligns with Maxwell's emphasis on both the heart and the hands of leadership—the inspirational and the practical.

Qualitative assessment tools in Conscious Leadership include feedback from employees, customers, and community members. These insights offer a window into the real-world impact of leadership decisions. Surveys, focus groups, and open forums are effective ways to gather this type of feedback. They reveal not just the numerical success of a venture but also its emotional and ethical resonance with stakeholders. As Maxwell noted, "Leaders must be close enough to relate to others, but far enough ahead to motivate them."

This proximity allows for genuine feedback, which is crucial for conscious leaders to gauge their influence.

Artificial Intelligence is rapidly transforming the leadership landscape, offering tools that enhance decision-making, streamline operations, and provide unprecedented access to data-driven insights. As shown in Figure 10.1: *The Role of AI in Leadership*, AI serves as a powerful enabler—augmenting human capabilities by supporting strategic analysis, automating routine tasks, and surfacing trends that inform more conscious, timely decisions. When aligned with emotionally intelligent leadership, AI can amplify a leader's capacity to engage stakeholders, personalize communication, and drive innovation at scale.

Despite its promise, AI has clear limitations when applied to leadership. As illustrated in *Figure 10.2,* AI lacks emotional context, ethical intuition, and the human sensitivity required to navigate complex interpersonal dynamics. Leadership is fundamentally relational—requiring empathy, moral judgment, and situational awareness that algorithms cannot replicate. Overreliance on AI can lead to depersonalized decision-making, unconscious bias, and ethical blind spots. Recognizing these boundaries ensures that AI remains a tool for augmentation, not a substitute for the wisdom and emotional intelligence that define Conscious Leadership.

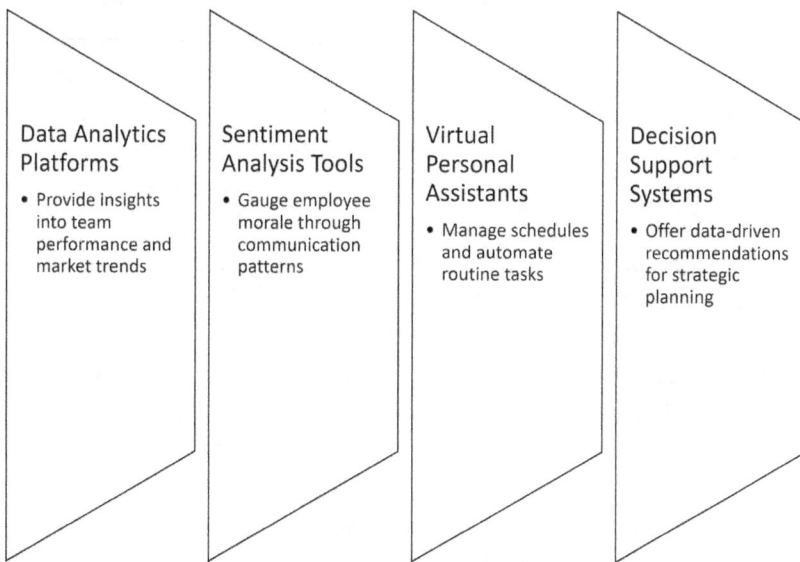

Data Analytics Platforms	Sentiment Analysis Tools	Virtual Personal Assistants	Decision Support Systems
• Provide insights into team performance and market trends	• Gauge employee morale through communication patterns	• Manage schedules and automate routine tasks	• Offer data-driven recommendations for strategic planning

FIGURE 10.1
Role of AI in Leadership.

Lack of Emotional Intelligence	• Inability to understand and respond to human emotions
Ethical Decision-Making Challenges	• Struggles with context based moral judgements
Creativity Constraints	• Limited capacity for innovative thinking beyond programmed data
Dependence on Quality Data	• Accuracy is contingent upon the input data's quality

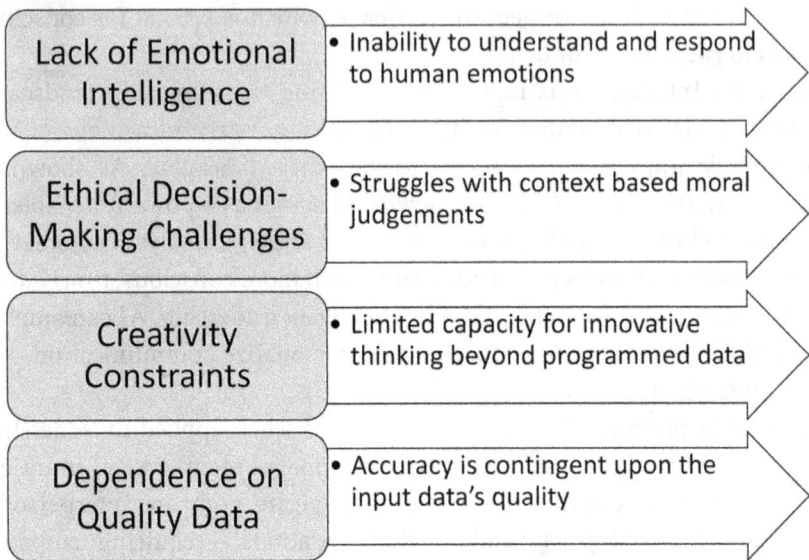

FIGURE 10.2
The Limitations of AI in Leadership.

As organizations begin to integrate AI tools into leadership workflows, conscious leaders must evaluate their utility not solely through technical capacity but through alignment with human-centered values. From predictive analytics and intelligent dashboards to sentiment analysis and automated coaching systems, these tools can enhance but never replace intentional, ethical decision-making. Figure 10.1 presents a visual map of AI-powered tools that support conscious leadership—highlighting use cases such as talent analytics, ethical risk scoring, and intelligent performance tracking.

While artificial intelligence can augment efficiency, automate decision-support processes, and analyze data at scale, it remains limited in areas requiring empathy, ethical nuance, and human intuition. These limitations underscore the importance of conscious leadership in a digital world. AI may process inputs, but it cannot yet mirror the depth of emotional intelligence or moral responsibility required in true leadership (see Figure 10.2). This diagram illustrates the key constraints of AI in leadership contexts—including ethical ambiguity, emotional absence, and contextual misinterpretation.

Quantitative tools are also indispensable. Data-driven metrics such as employee turnover rates, growth metrics, and market share can provide objective insights into the operational success of a leader's strategies. In Conscious Leadership, however, these metrics are interpreted through a lens of long-term sustainability and ethical practice. For example, a low employee turnover rate may not only indicate job satisfaction but also reflect a culture of trust and ethical treatment, aspects highly valued in Conscious Leadership.

Another critical tool is the 360-degree feedback mechanism. It involves collecting feedback about a leader from their subordinates, peers, and superiors. This comprehensive approach ensures that a leader's impact is evaluated from multiple perspectives, providing a holistic view of their effectiveness. This method aligns with Maxwell's concept that leadership effectiveness is determined not just by the leader's actions but also by the perceptions and reactions of those they lead.

In Conscious Leadership, the impact of decisions and actions is also measured over the long term. Short-term gains are weighed against long-term consequences, ensuring that today's successes do not become tomorrow's problems. This long-term perspective is vital in assessing the true impact of a leader's decisions, resonating with Maxwell's principle that "A leader is one who sees more than others see, who sees farther than others see, and who sees before others do."

THE ROLE OF FEEDBACK IN CONSCIOUS LEADERSHIP DEVELOPMENT

Feedback is a cornerstone in the development of Conscious Leadership. It provides leaders with insights into their actions' effects on others, fostering a cycle of continuous improvement and growth. Conscious leaders seek feedback not just to affirm their success but to genuinely understand their areas for development. This mirrors Maxwell's idea that growth is an ongoing process, where leaders are perpetual students of their own leadership journey.

In this context, feedback is both a mirror and a map. It reflects a leader's current effectiveness and charts a course for future development. Leaders must cultivate an environment where feedback is not only welcomed but actively sought. This involves creating a culture of trust where team members feel safe to express their thoughts and observations.

Effective feedback in Conscious Leadership is characterized by its constructiveness and focus on growth. It's not about assigning blame or highlighting shortcomings for their own sake. Instead, it's about identifying opportunities for improvement and development. Maxwell emphasized the importance of positive influence in leadership; similarly, feedback should be a tool for positive change.

Feedback mechanisms can be formal, like structured performance reviews, or informal, such as day-to-day interactions. Conscious leaders leverage both, understanding that formal mechanisms provide structured opportunities for reflection, while informal interactions offer real-time insights.

Moreover, conscious leaders recognize that feedback is a two-way street. They not only receive feedback but also provide it to their team members. This reciprocal approach reinforces a culture of mutual respect and continuous learning.

Continuous feedback in Conscious Leadership is not just a tool for assessment but a critical component of a leader's development. It enables leaders to align their actions with their values, ensures their growth is in tune with their team's needs, and fosters an environment of mutual respect and continuous improvement.

LONG-TERM IMPACT: CONSCIOUS LEADERSHIP AND ORGANIZATIONAL GROWTH

The Return on Investment (ROI) of Conscious Leadership can be profound, though not always easily quantifiable in traditional financial terms. This form of leadership yields dividends in areas like employee engagement, customer loyalty, and long-term sustainability, which ultimately contribute to financial success.

Conscious Leadership drives ROI by enhancing organizational reputation and trust. A leader's ethical stance and commitment to social responsibility resonate with customers and stakeholders, often leading to increased business and loyalty.

Moreover, conscious leaders invest in their employees' growth and well-being, leading to a more engaged and productive workforce. This investment reduces turnover costs and fosters a culture of excellence and innovation.

Additionally, Conscious Leadership's focus on sustainable practices can lead to cost savings and efficiencies over time. By prioritizing long-term sustainability over short-term gains, organizations can avoid future risks and expenses.

In summary, the ROI of Conscious Leadership is multi-dimensional, impacting not just the financial bottom line but also creating a lasting positive impact on the organization's culture, reputation, and sustainability.

CHAPTER 10 EXERCISES: LEADING THROUGH UNCERTAINTY AND CHANGE

These exercises focus on helping leaders navigate uncertainty, foster resilience, and lead teams through change with clarity and confidence. Each activity is individual, immediately applicable, and structured consistently with previous chapters.

Exercise 1: Personal Resilience Check-In

Objective: To assess your emotional and mental resilience in times of uncertainty and develop strategies to strengthen it.
   Instructions:

- **Reflect on a Recent Period of Uncertainty:**
  Identify a time when you faced uncertainty or change in your leadership role.
  - What emotions did you experience? How did you respond to the uncertainty?
  - **Identify Coping Mechanisms:** Write down the strategies you used to manage stress and maintain focus. Did they work? If not, what challenges arose?
- **Develop a Resilience Plan:**
  - List three practical ways to strengthen your resilience (e.g., mindfulness, seeking mentorship, structured problem-solving).
  - Identify one mindset shift that will help you better embrace change (e.g., viewing challenges as growth opportunities).
- **Apply and Reflect:**
  Over the next two weeks, practice your resilience strategies and track how they impact your ability to lead through uncertainty.

Exercise 2: Decision-Making under Uncertainty

Objective: To improve your ability to make confident, values-based decisions in uncertain situations.
   Instructions:

- **Recall a Recent Uncertain Decision:**
  Identify a leadership decision where you had incomplete information or high ambiguity.

- **Use the "3 Point Framework" for Decision-Making:**
  - What are the known facts? List out what is certain.
  - What are the possible outcomes? Consider best-case, worst-case, and most-likely scenarios.
  - What aligns with my leadership values? Make a decision based on principles, not fear.
- **Apply to an Upcoming Decision:**
  Use this framework for an impending decision and observe how it improves clarity and confidence.

Exercise 3: Guiding Your Team through Change

Objective: To develop a structured approach for leading teams through uncertainty while maintaining engagement.
  Instructions:

- **Choose a Current or Upcoming Organizational Change:**
  It could be a restructuring, a shift in strategy, or an industry disruption.
  - **Assess Team Concerns:**
    Consider how your team may feel about this change—uncertain, resistant, or disengaged? Write down their likely concerns.
- **Craft a Transparent Communication Plan:**
  - What is changing, and why?
  - How will this impact the team?
  - What support will be available?
- **Deliver Your Message:**
  Whether in a meeting or one to one conversations, communicate with transparency, empathy, and clarity.
- **Reflect on the Response:**
  Note team reactions and how your communication affected trust and morale. Adjust your approach for future changes.

Exercise 4: The Adaptability Challenge

Objective: To build the habit of embracing adaptability and fostering it within your team.
  Instructions:

- **Identify an Area Where You Struggle to Adapt:**
  Think about a process, system, or leadership style you resist changing.

- **Challenge Yourself to Experiment:**
  - Commit to one small change in your daily work routine (e.g., trying a new workflow, adjusting how you delegate, or leading a meeting differently).
  - Encourage your team to adopt a "test and learn" mindset by experimenting with new ideas.
- **Observe and Reflect:**
  - Did adopting change feel uncomfortable? What insights did you gain about adaptability?
  - How can you help your team become more comfortable with change?

Exercise 5: Creating Psychological Safety in Uncertain Times

Objective: To foster an environment where team members feel safe expressing concerns and ideas during periods of change.

   Instructions:

- **Assess Your Leadership Approach to Uncertainty:**
  - Do your team members feel safe voicing concerns?
  - Do you encourage open dialogue, or do people hesitate to speak up?
- **Commit to three Psychological Safety Practices:**
  - Ask open-ended questions in meetings ("What's on your mind?").
  - Acknowledge uncertainty honestly instead of pretending to have all the answers.
- Reframe mistakes as learning opportunities rather than failures.
- **Apply in Your Next Leadership Interaction:**
  Observe how these practices impact team trust and engagement.

Engage in relevant courses, workshops, or mentorship programs.

11

The Future of Conscious Leadership: A Global Perspective

In the discourse of Conscious Leadership, the significance of cultural diversity cannot be overstated. The future of Conscious Leadership demands a nuanced understanding and appreciation of leadership practices across various cultural contexts. This global perspective is not merely about adapting to different cultures but about deeply understanding and valuing the unique leadership paradigms each culture presents.

In Eastern cultures, for instance, leadership often focuses on collective harmony and the holistic well-being of the group. This approach is deeply rooted in philosophical teachings such as those of Confucius, emphasizing the moral integrity and communal responsibilities of leaders. A study by Chhokar, Brodbeck, and House in their book "Culture and Leadership Across the World: The GLOBE Book of In-Depth Studies of 25 Societies" highlights how Confucian values shape leadership in Asian cultures, emphasizing aspects like respect for hierarchy and a focus on group harmony.

Contrastingly, Western leadership paradigms, deeply influenced by ideals of individualism and liberalism, often emphasize personal achievement, innovation, and direct communication. As Hofstede's cultural dimensions theory suggests, cultures with high individualism, such as the United States, tend to foster leadership styles that are more participative and less hierarchical, encouraging autonomy and self-expression.

In African cultures, the concept of Ubuntu, which translates to "I am because we are," offers a profound lens through which to view leadership. This philosophy underscores the interconnectedness and interdependence of individuals within a community, and as a result, leadership is seen as a collective endeavor focused on the well-being of the community as a whole. A study by Mbigi and Maree in "Ubuntu: The Spirit of African

  DOI: 10.1201/9781003488705-11

Transformation Management" explores how Ubuntu influences leadership in African contexts, emphasizing values like empathy, community, and shared success.

The future of Conscious Leadership lies in integrating these diverse cultural insights into a cohesive approach that respects and leverages cultural differences. Leaders must cultivate a global mindset, one that is open, adaptable, and sensitive to the varied cultural landscapes in which they operate. As noted in the Harvard Business Review article "Cultural Agility: The Global Talent's Edge," by Paula Caligiuri, developing cultural agility—the ability to quickly, comfortably, and effectively work in different cultural contexts—is an essential skill for future leaders.

CONSCIOUS LEADERSHIP IN DIVERSE CULTURAL CONTEXTS

Leadership does not exist in a vacuum, and Conscious Leadership even less so. It thrives on diversity, drawing from a wellspring of cultural nuances. The conscious leader of today is both a student and teacher in a global classroom, where the syllabus is constantly rewritten by the evolving norms and values from countless societies.

Leadership, when viewed through the lens of cultural diversity, becomes a multifaceted gem, reflecting a spectrum of possibilities. A leader's consciousness is no longer judged by a single standard but by their ability to harmonize the varied cultural ethics, business practices, and communication styles into a coherent, respectful, and effective leadership strategy (Figure 11.1).

THE EVOLUTION OF LEADERSHIP IN THE DIGITAL AGE

As the world spins ever more rapidly into the digital future, leadership too evolves. The digital age demands a new kind of leader: one who is adept at navigating the cybernetic tides, connecting dots that span across the digital expanse, and harnessing the power of technology to foster genuine human connections.

The digital age has brought about transformative changes in leadership dynamics. The future of Conscious Leadership in this era will be shaped by

Leadership Principle	Eastern Leadership Style (Asia, Middle East)	Western Leadership Style (Europe, North America)	Shared Conscious Leadership Traits
Leadership Focus	Community-oriented, collective success	Individual-driven, innovation-focused	Ethical decision-making, purpose-driven leadership
Decision-Making Style	Consensus-based, hierarchical respect	Decentralized, participatory	Encourages collaboration & employee involvement
Communication Style	Indirect, high-context (implied meaning)	Direct, low-context (explicit meaning)	Emphasizes emotional intelligence and transparency
Conflict Resolution	Harmony-driven, avoiding open confrontation	Constructive debate, direct problem-solving	Empathy in resolving workplace disputes
Employee Motivation	Stability, long-term commitment	Growth, performance-driven incentives	Employee well-being and engagement focus
Work-Life Balance	Duty and loyalty to company, personal sacrifice	Individual work-life balance, autonomy	Mindfulness and wellness in leadership

FIGURE 11.1
Conscious Leadership across Cultures.

how leaders adapt to and integrate digital technologies while maintaining their focus on human-centric values.

In the digital realm, a key aspect for conscious leaders is to navigate the balance between technological efficiency and maintaining human connections. The rise of remote work, digital communication platforms, and artificial intelligence in decision-making processes has altered traditional leadership models. A conscious leader in the digital age must be tech-savvy yet also deeply aware of the importance of human interaction and ethical considerations.

A significant challenge in this era is digital ethics, encompassing issues like data privacy, cyber security, and the ethical use of AI. As leaders increasingly rely on data and algorithms to make decisions, there's a growing need to understand and address the ethical implications of these technologies. A study by the Capgemini Research Institute, "Why Addressing Ethical Questions in AI will Benefit Organizations," emphasizes the importance of ethical considerations in AI deployment and the role of leaders in ensuring these technologies are used responsibly.

Another aspect is the digital divide—the gap between those who have access to modern information and communication technology and those who do not. Conscious leaders must acknowledge and work toward bridging this divide, understanding that access to technology is increasingly becoming a determinant of social and economic opportunities. Research by the Pew Research Center on internet access and usage worldwide highlights the disparities in digital access and how they impact various communities, making it a crucial issue for leaders to address.

Moreover, the rapid pace of technological change requires leaders to be agile and adaptable. They must stay abreast of emerging technologies and trends, understanding their potential impact on business and society. The Harvard Business Review article "The Best Leaders Are Versatile Ones," by Robert B. Kaiser and Robert Hogan, discusses the importance of adaptability in leadership, especially in fast-changing environments like the digital age.

The future of Conscious Leadership in the digital age is about harnessing technology for the greater good while ensuring that it enhances rather than undermines human values. It's about leading with an understanding of the far-reaching implications of digital decisions and fostering a culture where technology serves to elevate human potential.

GLOBAL CHALLENGES AND CONSCIOUS LEADERSHIP RESPONSES

In the context of ever-mounting global challenges, the future of Conscious Leadership is pivotal. These challenges, including climate change, economic inequality, political instability, and social injustice, demand a leadership approach that is not only aware but actively engaged in creating positive change.

Conscious Leadership in response to climate change entails more than just implementing sustainable practices within an organization. It involves a broader vision of environmental stewardship and a commitment to sustainable development. Leaders must not only reduce the environmental impact of their operations but also innovate in ways that contribute to the overall health of the planet. A report by the United Nations Environment

Programme, "Emissions Gap Report 2020," underscores the urgent need for leadership in addressing climate change and reducing greenhouse gas emissions.

In addressing economic inequality, conscious leaders must engage in creating more inclusive and equitable economic systems. This involves ensuring fair labor practices, supporting fair trade, and investing in community development. The World Bank's report on "Poverty and Shared Prosperity 2020" highlights the growing disparity in wealth distribution and the role of leadership in addressing economic inequalities.

Political instability and social injustice are other critical areas where Conscious Leadership is needed. Leaders must advocate for democratic principles, human rights, and social justice. They have a role in fostering dialogue, understanding, and collaboration across political and social divides. The work of the Institute for Economics and Peace, particularly the "Global Peace Index," provides insights into how political stability and peace are crucial for sustainable development and the role leaders play in achieving these goals.

In the face of these challenges, conscious leaders are called to be visionaries and change agents, leading with empathy, integrity, and a commitment to the greater good. They must develop strategies that are not only effective in the short term but sustainable in the long term, ensuring that their leadership leaves a positive legacy for future generations.

The future of Conscious Leadership lies in its ability to respond to these global challenges with innovative solutions, moral courage, and a deep sense of responsibility toward the planet and its inhabitants. It's about creating a world where leadership is not just a position of power but a force for good, driving positive change in every corner of the globe.

VISIONS OF THE FUTURE: WHERE CONSCIOUS LEADERSHIP IS HEADED

As we project into the future, the trajectory of Conscious Leadership suggests a transformative shift in the way leadership is perceived and practiced globally. This evolution is not just a trend but a paradigm shift toward a more holistic, inclusive, and sustainable approach to leadership.

The future of Conscious Leadership is marked by a greater emphasis on global citizenship and sustainability. Leaders will increasingly recognize their role in addressing global issues, transcending beyond the confines of their organizations or local communities. This shift is exemplified in the United Nations' Sustainable Development Goals (SDGs), which call for global partnership and collaborative efforts in solving the world's most pressing problems. Conscious leaders will align their strategies and operations with these goals, contributing to a more sustainable and equitable world.

Another defining feature of future Conscious Leadership is the integration of emotional intelligence and mindfulness into leadership practices. As organizations face increasingly complex challenges, the ability of leaders to manage their emotions and make empathetic, mindful decisions becomes crucial. Research by Daniel Goleman, a psychologist and author renowned for his work on emotional intelligence, highlights its significance in effective leadership. Leaders who are emotionally intelligent foster better team dynamics, higher employee engagement, and more resilient organizations.

Innovation and adaptability will also be hallmarks of Conscious Leadership in the future. The rapid pace of technological advancement and changing global dynamics necessitate leaders who are not only open to change but actively embrace and drive it. They must foster a culture of innovation within their organizations, encouraging creative thinking and experimentation.

Moreover, the future of Conscious Leadership will see a stronger focus on ethical decision-making and social responsibility. Leaders will be expected to uphold high ethical standards and be accountable for the social and environmental impact of their decisions. This ethical leadership approach aligns with the growing demand from consumers, employees, and stakeholders for transparency, accountability, and social responsibility in business practices.

Finally, the future of Conscious Leadership is inclusive, embracing diversity in all its forms. Leaders will recognize the value of diverse perspectives and experiences, creating environments where different voices are heard and valued. This inclusivity not only enriches decision-making processes but also reflects the diverse world in which organizations operate.

In essence, the future of Conscious Leadership is about leading with a purpose that extends beyond profit and personal success. It's about nurturing a leadership style that is empathetic, ethical, innovative, and globally minded, committed to creating a positive impact in the world.

THE GLOBAL CONSCIOUS LEADERSHIP NETWORK AND ITS IMPACT

The concept of a Global Conscious Leadership Network represents a progressive step toward a unified and effective approach to leadership on a worldwide scale. This network, envisioned as a collaborative and inclusive platform, brings together leaders from various sectors, cultures, and regions to address global challenges through a lens of consciousness and ethical responsibility.

The impact of such a network is multi-dimensional:

Sharing Best Practices and Innovation: A key benefit of this network is the facilitation of knowledge exchange and the sharing of best practices among leaders. By learning from diverse experiences and successes, leaders can adopt and adapt strategies that have proven effective in different contexts. This collaboration fosters innovation, as leaders are exposed to a variety of approaches and ideas that they may not encounter within their usual spheres. The Harvard Business Review's article, "Collaborative Overload" by Cross, Rebele, and Grant, discusses the importance and challenges of collaboration in modern organizations, emphasizing the value of diverse inputs and shared learning.

Advocacy and Influence: The network serves as a powerful collective voice advocating for sustainable and ethical practices in business and governance. United in their commitment to Conscious Leadership principles, this network can influence policy, drive social change, and raise awareness about critical issues like climate change, social justice, and ethical business practices. As demonstrated in the World Economic Forum's reports, collective leadership action can significantly impact policy decisions and public opinion.

Mentorship and Development of Future Leaders: Another crucial role of this network is the cultivation and mentorship of the next generation of leaders. Through mentorship programs, leadership development initiatives, and educational resources, experienced leaders can pass on their knowledge and insights, nurturing a new breed of conscious leaders. This aspect aligns with the findings in "Mentoring Executives and Directors" by Clutterbuck and Ragins, which highlights the importance of mentorship in leadership development.

Global and Cultural Perspective: The network enhances the global and cultural perspective of its members. By bringing together leaders from different backgrounds, the network fosters a deeper understanding of cultural nuances in leadership, encouraging practices that are respectful and effective across cultural boundaries. In their book "Riding the Waves of Culture: Understanding Diversity in Global Business," Trompenaars and

Hampden-Turner explore the significance of cultural understanding in international business, a concept that is central to the network's ethos.

Collective Action and Impact: Perhaps the most significant impact of the Global Conscious Leadership Network is its capacity for collective action. By pooling resources, expertise, and influence, the network can undertake initiatives and projects that have a substantial and lasting impact on global issues. This collective approach to leadership is increasingly seen as essential in addressing complex, interconnected challenges that no single leader or organization can solve alone.

In summary, the Global Conscious Leadership Network symbolizes a shift toward more collaborative, ethical, and globally Conscious Leadership. Its impact extends beyond individual organizations, fostering a worldwide movement of leaders committed to positive change and sustainable development (Figure 11.2).

FIGURE 11.2
The Global Conscious Leadership Network.

CHAPTER 11 EXERCISES: LEADING HIGH-PERFORMING TEAMS

These exercises focus on developing trust, collaboration, accountability, and motivation within high-performing teams. Each activity is structured for individual application, immediately actionable, and aligned with Conscious Leadership principles.

Exercise 1: The Trust Accelerator

Objective: To identify and strengthen trust-building behaviors within your team.

  Instructions:

1. **Assess Your Team's Current Trust Level:**
   - On a scale of 1–5, rate how much trust exists between you and your team. What behaviors contribute to this level of trust?
   - What actions or habits weaken trust?
2. **Identify a Trust-Building Action:**
   Choose one practical behavior to implement this week. Examples:
   - Be more transparent in decision-making.
   - Follow through on commitments more consistently. Give team members more autonomy and ownership.
3. **Apply and Observe:**
   Implement your trust-building action and note how the team responds.
4. **Reflect and Adjust:**
   Did this action strengthen trust? What will you continue doing moving forward?

Exercise 2: The Collaboration Audit

Objective: To evaluate team collaboration and remove barriers to effective teamwork.

  Instructions:

- **Assess Current Collaboration:**
  - Do team members share information openly, or do silos exist? Are decisions made collectively, or do a few voices dominate? Does the team value diverse perspectives?

- **Identify a Collaboration Challenge:**
  - What is one obstacle preventing stronger teamwork?
- **Implement a Solution:**
  Take conscious action to improve team collaboration. Examples:
  - Introduce a structured brainstorming session to include more voices. Facilitate discussion on team norms to strengthen communication. Establish clearer cross-functional workflows.
- **Observe and Reflect:**
  After implementing the change, assess its impact and adjust as needed.

Exercise 3: The Accountability Check

Objective: To ensure clear expectations and ownership within your team.
  Instructions:

1. **Review Your Accountability Approach:**
   - Do team members understand their individual roles and responsibilities?
   - How do you currently hold people accountable without micromanaging?
   - Are expectations clearly communicated?
2. **Select a Team Member Who Needs More Clarity:**
   - Choose an individual who may be struggling with accountability and identify what needs to be reinforced.
3. **Have an Alignment Conversation:**
   - Restate their responsibilities and goals clearly.
   - **Ask for their input:** "How do you see your role in contributing to our team's success?"
   - Offer support while reinforcing ownership of outcomes.
4. **Reflect on Results:**
   - Did they gain clarity and take more responsibility?
   - How can you improve how you set expectations in the future?

Exercise 4: Motivating Your Team without Micromanaging

Objective: To strengthen intrinsic motivation and team engagement.
  Instructions:

1. Identify What Motivates Your Team Members:

    a. Observe what drives each person—is it growth opportunities, autonomy, recognition, or purpose-driven work?

    b. Are there individuals who seem disengaged?

2. Adjust Your Leadership Style to Match Their Motivators:

    a. If someone thrives on autonomy, give them more freedom in decision-making.

    b. If recognition is important, acknowledge their contributions publicly.

    c. If they seek purpose, connect their tasks to a larger mission.

3. Apply and Observe: Make these small shifts and assess whether engagement and motivation improve.

Exercise 5: The Strengths-Based Leadership Challenge

Objective: To maximize team performance by leveraging individual strengths.

  Instructions:

1. **Assess Your Team's Strengths:**

    a. Write down each team member's greatest strength (e.g., analytical thinking, creativity, execution).

    b. Compare their strengths with their current responsibilities.

2. **Identify a Strengths Misalignment:**

    a. Is anyone's strength underutilized? Redesign Responsibilities:

    b. Assign a new challenge or project that aligns with their strengths. Allow someone to mentor or train others in their area of expertise.

3. **Measure the Impact:**

    a. Did they perform better?

    b. Did this change improve overall team effectiveness?

4. What adjustments should be made to further leverage strengths?

Engage in relevant courses, workshops, or mentorship programs.

12

The Role of Intuition in Leadership Decisions

INTUITION VS. ANALYSIS: FINDING THE BALANCE

In the realm of leadership, the interplay between intuition and analysis is a critical aspect of decision-making. While analysis relies on data, evidence, and logical reasoning, intuition is about gut feelings and instincts. The future of conscious leadership involves finding a delicate balance between these two, leveraging the strengths of both to make informed and insightful decisions.

Intuitive decision-making in leadership is often viewed as an innate skill, a kind of sixth sense that some leaders possess. However, this perspective overlooks the complexity of intuition, which is, in many ways, a cognitive process informed by past experiences, knowledge, and subconscious cues. Gary Klein's research, as presented in his book "Sources of Power: How People Make Decisions," delves into how intuition works in high-stakes environments, showing that it is often a rapid, yet informed, synthesis of information.

However, analytical decision-making is grounded in data and logical reasoning. It involves a systematic examination of facts, trends, and variables, often using tools like SWOT analysis or cost-benefit analysis. This methodical approach is crucial in complex scenarios where decisions have far-reaching consequences. Daniel Kahneman's work, particularly in "Thinking, Fast and Slow," highlights the importance of slow, deliberate thinking in contrast to fast, intuitive judgments.

The challenge for conscious leaders is to find the right balance between intuition and analysis. This balance depends on the context of the decision, the urgency of the situation, and the leader's personal strengths and experiences. In some scenarios, relying on intuition can lead to rapid, effective

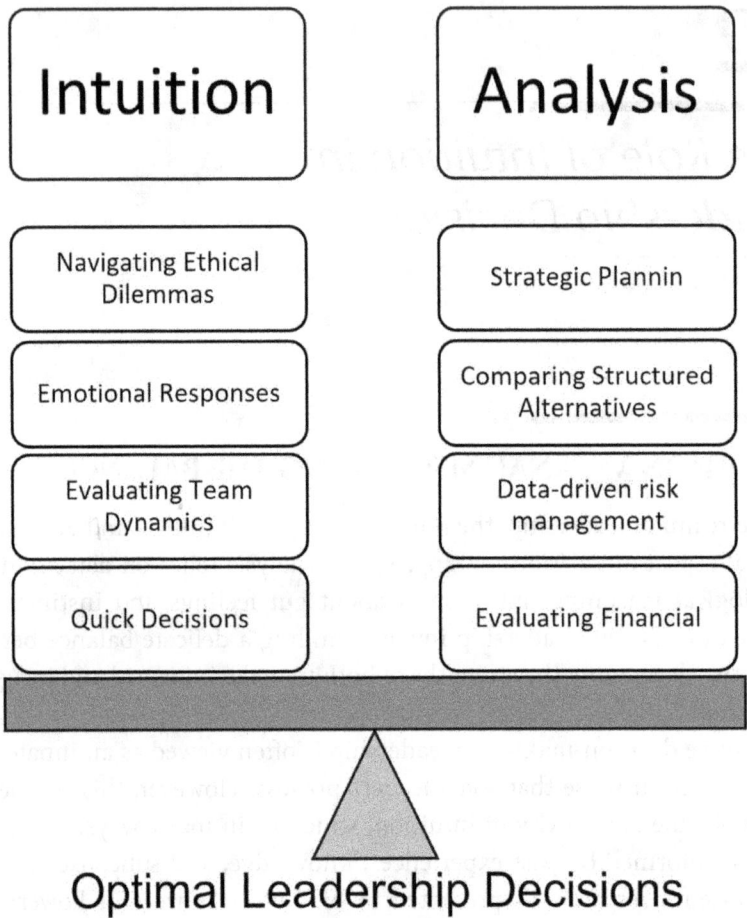

FIGURE 12.1
Balancing Intuition and Analysis.

decision-making, while in others, a more analytical approach might be necessary. The key is to develop the ability to discern which approach is most suitable for each situation (Figure 12.1).

CULTIVATING INTUITIVE SKILLS FOR BETTER DECISION-MAKING

Intuition, often referred to as 'gut feeling,' plays a significant role in leadership decision-making. However, unlike analytical skills, which can be learned and honed through education and practice, intuition is more elusive. It involves a subconscious process where experience, knowledge, and environmental cues converge to produce insights that are not immediately obvious. The cultivation of intuitive skills in leadership is therefore about refining one's ability to recognize and interpret these subconscious cues.

One way leaders can cultivate their intuitive skills is through reflective practice. This involves regularly taking time to reflect on decisions, actions, and their outcomes. Such reflection enables leaders to identify patterns in their decision-making processes, including instances where intuition led to successful outcomes. This practice is akin to the concept of 'reflective practice' in Donald Schön's book "The Reflective Practitioner," which emphasizes the importance of reflecting on one's actions to improve one's professional practice.

Another approach is to consciously expose oneself to a wide range of experiences and perspectives. This broad exposure enhances one's ability to make intuitive judgments by enriching the subconscious pool of knowledge and experience from which intuitive insights are drawn. In her book "Intuition: Its Powers and Perils," David G. Myers highlights how varied experiences contribute to the development of intuition.

Additionally, mindfulness and meditation can be effective tools for cultivating intuition. These practices help in quieting the mind, allowing leaders to be more attuned to their inner thoughts and feelings. As they become more mindful, they can better sense the subtle intuitive cues that often go unnoticed in the hustle of daily life. Research on mindfulness, such as that presented in "The Mindful Brain" by Daniel J. Siegel, has shown its effectiveness in enhancing self-awareness and intuition.

Encouraging open dialogue and fostering a culture of diversity within the organization also aids in developing intuition. Exposure to different perspectives and ideas challenges leaders to think beyond their standard frameworks, thereby enriching their intuitive capabilities.

THE SCIENCE BEHIND INTUITION IN LEADERSHIP

The concept of intuition in leadership, often seen as a nebulous or mystical quality, is actually grounded in cognitive science. Intuition is a rapid, unconscious process where the brain synthesizes accumulated knowledge, past experiences, and environmental cues to arrive at decisions. It's a form of cognitive processing that is faster and less structured than analytical thinking but can be equally powerful in decision-making.

Neuroscientific research has shed light on the brain mechanisms underlying intuition. Studies using functional magnetic resonance imaging (fMRI) have shown that intuition involves several brain regions, including the prefrontal cortex, which is associated with complex decision-making and problem-solving. A study by Bechara and Damasio, discussed in "Descartes' Error: Emotion, Reason, and the Human Brain," suggests that emotional responses play a key role in intuitive decision-making, highlighting the interplay between emotion and cognition.

Psychological research also supports the role of intuition in leadership. Daniel Kahneman and Amos Tversky's work on heuristics and biases illustrates how intuitive judgments, while sometimes prone to errors, can be incredibly efficient and effective in certain scenarios. Their research, presented in the book "Judgment under Uncertainty: Heuristics and Biases," outlines various cognitive shortcuts that our brain uses, demonstrating the underlying processes of intuitive thinking.

Further, the concept of 'thin-slicing,' popularized by Malcolm Gladwell in his book "Blink: The Power of Thinking Without Thinking," refers to the ability to find patterns in events based only on 'thin slices' or small amounts of information. This ability is a crucial aspect of intuition in leadership, where leaders often have to make quick decisions with limited information.

In summary, the science behind intuition in leadership reveals that it is a legitimate and valuable cognitive process. It is not about guessing or relying on mystical insights but about harnessing the power of the brain's ability to process information rapidly and unconsciously. This understanding is crucial for leaders who aim to balance intuitive and analytical decision-making in their leadership approach.

STORIES OF INTUITION IN LEADERSHIP SUCCESSES AND FAILURES

The impact of intuition in leadership can be best understood through real-world stories that illustrate both its successes and failures. These stories provide valuable insights into how intuition, when used effectively, can lead to remarkable outcomes, and conversely, when misjudged, can result in significant missteps.

One notable success story is that of a technology CEO who decided to invest in an innovative but risky new product based largely on intuition. Despite skepticism from the board and lack of substantial market data, the CEO's gut feeling was that this product would meet an emerging need. This intuition was based on years of industry experience and a deep understanding of customer behavior. The product turned out to be a massive success, revolutionizing the market and securing the company's position as an industry leader. This scenario echoes Steve Jobs' approach at Apple, where many of his successful decisions were driven by intuition rather than traditional market analysis.

On the flip side, there are stories of intuition leading to failure, such as a CEO who decided to merge with another company based on a gut feeling that it would create a powerful synergy. However, this decision was made without adequate due diligence and a thorough analysis of cultural compatibility between the two organizations. The result was a disastrous merger, leading to significant financial losses and cultural clashes. This example highlights the risks of relying solely on intuition without substantiating it with analysis and data.

These stories underscore the dual nature of intuition in leadership. When aligned with deep industry knowledge, experience, and a clear understanding of the context, intuition can lead to groundbreaking decisions. However, when based on superficial impressions or used in isolation from data and analysis, it can lead to costly mistakes.

The key takeaway for leaders is to recognize the power of intuition while also understanding its limitations. Integrating intuition with analytical thinking, seeking diverse perspectives, and being aware of personal biases can help in making more balanced and informed decisions (Figure 12.2).

Successful Intuitive Decisions	*Failed Intuitive Decisions*
Intuitive Innovation in Leadership Tech CEO trusted their gut and approved high risk technology launch **Outcome:** Revolutionized the industry instant success	**Ignoring Market Data in Expansion** A CEO expanded into a new market purely on instinct, dismissing research and forecasting. **Outcome:** Expansion failed due to regulatory challenges and lack of demand
Crisis Leadership Success Leader relied on emotional intelligence rather than corporate policies to resolve internal dispute **Outcome:** Team regained trust and increased communication	**Flawed Merger Decision** Company leader merged 2 organizations based on a gut feeling about synergy without cultural assessment **Outcome:** Employee conflicts and financial instability led to failure
Successful Talent Recognition A leader promoted a candidate based on potential and instinct rather than strict performance metrics **Outcome:** Employee excelled, driving innovation and engagement	**Overconfidence in Hiring** Leader hired an executive purely based on intuition without verifying references **Outcome:** The hire underperformed, leading to misalignment and team instability

FIGURE 12.2
Intuition in Leadership Success and Failure Stories.

INTEGRATING INTUITION INTO LEADERSHIP DEVELOPMENT PROGRAMS

Integrating intuition into leadership development programs is crucial for cultivating well-rounded leaders who can navigate complex and uncertain environments effectively. While traditional leadership programs often focus on developing analytical and strategic skills, incorporating intuition training can provide leaders with a more comprehensive toolkit for decision-making.

One approach to integrating intuition in leadership development is through experiential learning. Experiential learning activities, such as simulations, role-playing, and case studies, can help leaders practice relying on their intuition in controlled, reflective environments. These activities mimic real-life scenarios where leaders must make quick decisions based on limited information, helping them to recognize and trust their intuitive insights. Kolb's Experiential Learning Theory, which emphasizes the importance of experience in the learning process, supports this approach.

Mentorship and coaching are also effective in developing intuitive skills. Experienced mentors can share insights on how they have used intuition in their leadership journey, providing practical examples and guidance. Coaching sessions can focus on helping leaders to tune into their inner thoughts and feelings, recognize intuitive cues, and understand how their intuition influences their decision-making.

Mindfulness and meditation training can also be incorporated into leadership development programs to enhance intuitive abilities. These practices help in cultivating self-awareness and attentiveness to the present moment, key components of intuitive thinking. Research, such as that presented in "The Mindful Leader" by Michael Bunting, has shown the benefits of mindfulness in leadership, including improved decision-making and increased emotional intelligence.

Additionally, encouraging reflective practices, such as journaling or debriefing sessions, can help leaders analyze their intuitive decisions and learn from them. Reflective practices enable leaders to understand the outcomes of their intuitive choices, refine their intuitive skills, and develop a more conscious approach to using intuition in decision-making.

In summary, integrating intuition into leadership development programs involves a combination of experiential learning, mentorship, mindfulness practices, and reflective exercises. By doing so, leadership programs can produce leaders who are not only analytically sound but also intuitively attuned, capable of making well-rounded decisions in today's complex and fast-paced world.

CHAPTER 12 EXERCISES: NAVIGATING ETHICAL DILEMMAS IN LEADERSHIP

These exercises are designed to enhance your ability to recognize, analyze, and address ethical challenges in leadership. By engaging in these activities, you'll strengthen your ethical decision-making skills and promote a culture of integrity within your organization.

Exercise 1: Ethical Self-reflection

Objective: To increase self-awareness regarding your ethical beliefs and how they influence your leadership decisions.
  Instructions:

- **Identify Core Ethical Values:**
  - List the top five ethical principles that guide your personal and professional life (e.g., honesty, fairness, accountability).
- **Reflect on Past Decisions:**
  - Recall a recent leadership decision where you faced an ethical dilemma. Analyze how your core values influenced your choice and the outcome.
- **Assess Alignment:**
  - Evaluate whether your actions aligned with your stated values.
  - Identify any discrepancies and consider their impact on your leadership effectiveness.
- **Plan for Improvement:**
  - Determine steps to ensure future decisions consistently reflect your ethical standards.

Exercise 2: Ethical Decision-Making Framework

Objective: To develop a structured approach for resolving ethical dilemmas in leadership.

Instructions:

1. **Learn an Ethical Framework:**
   a. Familiarize yourself with an ethical decision-making model, such as the PLUS model (Policies, Legal, Universal, Self).
2. **Apply the Framework:**
   a. Identify a current or potential ethical issue in your organization. Use the chosen framework to analyze the situation systematically.
3. **Make a Decision:**
   a. Based on your analysis, decide on the most ethical course of action.
4. **Implement and Reflect:**
   a. Execute your decision and later reflect on its effectiveness and any lessons learned.

Exercise 3: Stakeholder Impact Assessment

Objective: To evaluate the effects of your decisions on various stakeholders, promoting ethical leadership.

Instructions:

1. **Identify Stakeholders:**
   a. List all parties affected by a recent significant decision (e.g., employees, customers, community).
2. **Assess Impact:**
   a. For each stakeholder, analyze the positive and negative consequences of the decision.
3. **Reflect on Findings:**
   a. Consider whether the decision upheld ethical standards concerning stakeholder interests.
4. **Develop Strategies:**
   a. Plan how to mitigate negative impacts and enhance positive outcomes in future decisions.

Exercise 4: Ethical Culture Evaluation

Objective: To assess and improve the ethical climate within your team or organization.

Instructions:

- **Evaluate Current Culture:**
  - Observe and note behaviors, communications, and policies that reflect the organization's ethical standards.
- **Gather Feedback:**
  - Conduct anonymous surveys or discussions to understand employees' perceptions of the ethical environment.
- **Identify Areas for Improvement:**
  - Analyze feedback to pinpoint weaknesses or gaps in the ethical culture.
- **Implement Enhancements:**
  - Develop and execute action plans to strengthen ethical practices, such as training programs or policy revisions.

Exercise 5: Role-Playing Ethical Scenarios

Objective: To practice handling ethical dilemmas through simulated situations, enhancing preparedness and response strategies.

Instructions:

1. **Create Ethical Scenarios:**
   a. Develop realistic situations relevant to your industry where ethical dilemmas may arise.
2. **Organize Role-Playing Sessions:**
   a. With colleagues, assign roles and act out the scenarios, exploring different perspectives and solutions.
3. **Debrief and Discuss:**
   a. After each role-play, discuss what was learned, the challenges faced, and effective resolution strategies.
4. **Apply Insights:**
   a. Use the insights gained to inform real-life ethical decision-making and policy development.

Engage in relevant courses, workshops, or mentorship programs.

13

Navigating Change and Uncertainty with Conscious Leadership

UNDERSTANDING THE NATURE OF CHANGE AND UNCERTAINTY

In the journey of Conscious Leadership, navigating change and uncertainty is a fundamental aspect. Change, in its very essence, is the only constant in both life and business. It brings with it opportunities as well as challenges. Understanding the nature of change and uncertainty is crucial for leaders to adapt and thrive in an ever-evolving landscape.

Change can be external, driven by factors such as technological advancements, market dynamics, or global events. Alternatively, it can be internal, stemming from organizational restructuring, shifts in company culture, or leadership changes. Uncertainty often accompanies change, characterized by a lack of predictability and the potential for unexpected outcomes.

The nature of change is complex and multifaceted. It can be gradual or sudden, predictable or unforeseen. The Harvard Business Review article, "Leading Change: Why Transformation Efforts Fail" by John P. Kotter, discusses how leaders often underestimate the complexity of change and the resistance it can evoke. Kotter emphasizes the need for a clear vision and strategy to guide change initiatives.

Uncertainty, however, demands a different set of skills from leaders. It requires the ability to make decisions in the absence of complete information, to be flexible and adaptable, and to maintain a positive outlook even when the path ahead is unclear. As noted in the book "Comfortable with Uncertainty" by Pema Chödrön, leaders must learn to embrace uncertainty as an integral part of the change process.

Understanding change and uncertainty involves recognizing their inherent nature and preparing oneself and the organization to navigate through

DOI: 10.1201/9781003488705-13

them. It requires a balance of strategic planning and the ability to remain agile and responsive.

MINDSETS FOR LEADING THROUGH AMBIGUITY

Leadership in an environment of change and uncertainty demands a specific mindset. John C. Maxwell often emphasizes the importance of cultivating the right mental framework, and in this section, we'll explore the mindsets that empower leaders to navigate ambiguity effectively.

Adaptive Mindset: The adaptive mindset is rooted in the belief that change is a constant, and leaders must be flexible and open to new possibilities. It complements the growth mindset by viewing change as an opportunity for growth and learning. Leaders with this mindset embrace change and are willing to adjust their strategies and tactics as needed. Skills associated with the adaptive mindset include:

- **Agility:** The ability to respond quickly and effectively to changing circumstances.
- **Creativity:** The capacity to think outside the box and generate innovative solutions.
- **Anticipation:** Being proactive in anticipating and preparing for changes in the environment.
- **Growth Mindset:** This mindset sees challenges as opportunities for personal and organizational development. It complements the adaptive mindset by emphasizing the positive aspects of change. Leaders with a growth mindset inspire their teams to embrace challenges and learn from them.

Skills associated with the growth mindset include:

- **Passion for Learning:** A commitment to continuous learning and improvement.
- **Inspirational Leadership:** The ability to motivate and encourage others to strive for excellence. Long-term Perspective: Focusing on the big picture and long-term goals.
- **Resilient Mindset:** Resilience is the ability to bounce back from setbacks and adversity. While it may seem contradictory to the growth mindset

when dealing with setbacks, it complements the adaptive mindset by providing the strength to endure and persevere.

Skills associated with the resilient mindset include:

Emotional Intelligence: The capacity to understand and manage one's emotions and those of others.

Stress Management: Techniques for coping with stress and maintaining composure under pressure.

Determination: The commitment to staying the course even when faced with challenges.

Inclusive Mindset: Inclusivity values diverse perspectives and fosters collaboration. It complements the adaptive and growth mindsets by encouraging innovation through the integration of different viewpoints.

Skills associated with the inclusive mindset include:

Active Listening: The ability to truly hear and understand others' perspectives. Empathy: The capacity to recognize and relate to the feelings and experiences of others.

Team Building: The skill of assembling and leading diverse teams effectively.

Visionary Mindset: A clear vision provides direction and purpose during uncertain times (Figure 13.1).

It complements the growth mindset by inspiring confidence in the future. While it may appear contradictory to the adaptive mindset, a visionary leader can adapt their approach while staying true to their overarching vision.

Skills associated with the visionary mindset include:

Strategic Thinking: The ability to develop and execute a long-term strategy.

Communication: Effectively conveying the vision to inspire and align the team.

Inspiration: Motivating others to commit to the vision and work toward its realization.

Servant Leadership Mindset: Servant Leadership prioritizes the well-being of team members and fosters collaboration. It complements the inclusive mindset by focusing on serving others.

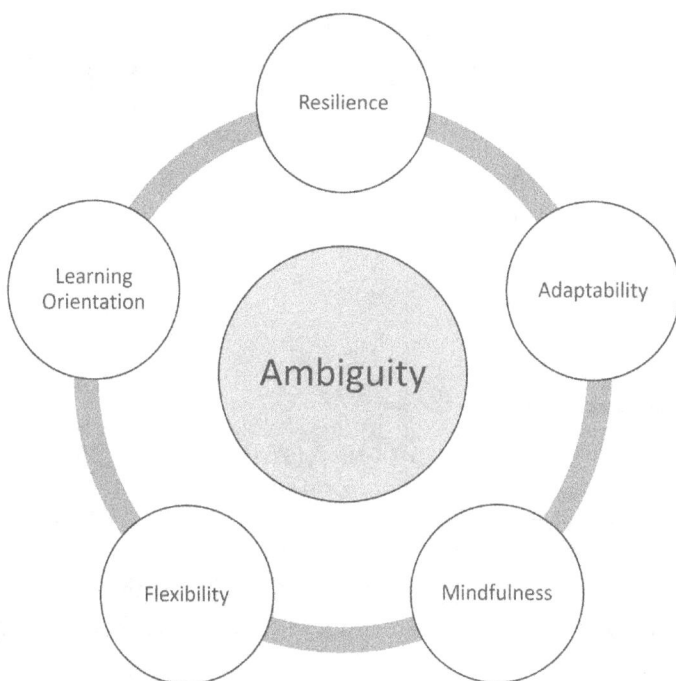

FIGURE 13.1
Mindsets for Leading through Ambiguity.

While it may seem contradictory to the visionary mindset if leaders prioritize serving their team without providing clear direction, a balance can be achieved. Skills associated with the Servant Leadership mindset include:

Empathy: Understanding and addressing the needs and concerns of team members.

Humility: Recognizing one's limitations and valuing the contributions of others.

Empowerment: Enabling team members to take ownership and contribute to the team's success.

These leadership mindsets are not mutually exclusive; rather, they offer a holistic approach to navigating change and uncertainty. Effective leaders can adapt and blend these mindsets based on the specific challenges they face, ultimately leading their teams to success in an ever-evolving landscape.

In essence, these leadership mindsets are not mutually exclusive but rather interconnected. Effective leaders blend these mindsets based on the specific context and challenges they face. This holistic approach involves using these mindsets as a toolkit, selecting the right one for the situation at hand, and seamlessly transitioning between them as needed. It recognizes that no single mindset is sufficient for all circumstances.

By embracing this comprehensive approach to leadership, leaders can navigate change and uncertainty with confidence, adaptability, and resilience while fostering an inclusive and purpose-driven culture within their teams. This approach empowers leaders to not only survive but thrive in the face of change and uncertainty.

TOOLS AND STRATEGIES FOR ADAPTIVE LEADERSHIP

Adaptive leadership is the cornerstone of Conscious Leadership in an ever-changing world. To effectively lead through change and uncertainty, leaders need a toolkit of tools and strategies that align with John C. Maxwell's wisdom, "Leadership is not about being in charge. It is about taking care of those in your charge."

Here are some essential tools and strategies for adaptive leadership:

Scenario Planning: Leaders employ scenario planning to envision multiple potential future scenarios and develop strategies for each. This proactive approach enables leaders to anticipate change and respond strategically, aligning with the adaptive and visionary mindsets.

Agile Frameworks: Derived from software development, agile methodologies emphasize adaptability, collaboration, and iterative progress. Leaders can implement agile practices to foster adaptability within their teams, promoting an agile and responsive culture.

Change Communication: Effective communication during times of change is crucial. Leaders should keep their teams informed, engaged, and motivated through transparent and empathetic communication, aligning with the inclusive mindset.

Learning and Development Programs: A growth mindset thrives on learning and development opportunities. Leaders invest in training and educational programs to ensure their teams possess the skills needed to adapt to new challenges, fostering personal and organizational growth.

Resilience Training: Building resilience in teams is a strategic advantage. Leaders promote resilience through workshops and support programs, strengthening their team's ability to bounce back from setbacks.

Innovation Hubs: Creating spaces or initiatives dedicated to innovation encourages teams to explore new ideas and solutions. This approach fosters an adaptive and growth-oriented culture that encourages creative thinking.

Crisis Management Plans: Preparedness is essential. Leaders should have well-defined crisis management plans in place, ensuring a structured response to unexpected challenges and demonstrating a resilient mindset.

Empowerment and Delegation: Leaders empower team members by delegating decision-making authority, enabling faster responses to changing circumstances. This approach aligns with the principles of Servant Leadership.

Data and Analytics: Leveraging data and analytics helps leaders make informed decisions in real-time, supporting the adaptive mindset by providing valuable insights for strategic adjustments.

Mentorship and Coaching: Mentorship and coaching programs promote personal growth and development within teams, reinforcing the growth mindset by fostering continuous learning.

These tools and strategies work in harmony to equip leaders and their teams for adaptive leadership. Leaders can blend these approaches as needed to address the specific challenges they face, creating a resilient, adaptable, and motivated team ready to thrive in the face of change and uncertainty.

CASE STUDIES IN CHANGE MANAGEMENT: A CONSCIOUS APPROACH

To truly understand how Conscious Leadership operates in the realm of change management and uncertainty, we turn to real-world case studies. Examining these cases provides invaluable insights into the application of Conscious Leadership principles in challenging circumstances.

IBM's Transformation under Lou Gerstner

In the early 1990s, IBM was on the brink of bankruptcy, facing a rapidly changing technology landscape. Lou Gerstner, the newly appointed CEO, embarked on a transformative journey that showcased a visionary mindset.

Key Elements of Transformation

Customer-Centric Approach: Gerstner prioritized understanding and addressing customer needs. He shifted the company's focus from products to solutions, aligning IBM with the changing market.

Valuing Employee Expertise: Gerstner recognized the wealth of knowledge within IBM's workforce. He engaged employees in decision-making and tapped into their expertise to drive innovation.

Strategic Direction: Under Gerstner's leadership, IBM regained its market leadership by embracing the growth mindset. The company invested in research and development, creating new technologies and solutions.

Netflix's Evolution from DVD Rentals to Streaming

Reed Hastings, the co-founder of Netflix, demonstrated adaptive leadership in response to changing consumer behavior and technological advancements.

Key Elements of Evolution

Recognizing Market Shifts: Hastings observed the shift from physical DVD rentals to digital streaming. He acknowledged that embracing this change was essential for the company's survival.

Content Creation: Netflix ventured into producing original content, further emphasizing adaptability. This move allowed the company to stand out in the crowded streaming market.

Data-Driven Decisions: Netflix's use of data and analytics aligned with an adaptive mindset. The company leveraged viewer preferences to inform content creation and recommendations.

Apple's Resurgence under Steve Jobs

Steve Jobs' return to Apple marked a remarkable turnaround, exemplifying visionary leadership principles.

Key Elements of Resurgence

Innovation and Design: Jobs' visionary mindset was evident in Apple's relentless pursuit of innovation and design excellence. Products like the iPhone and iPad transformed entire industries.

Customer Experience: Apple focused on providing exceptional customer experiences, aligning with the growth mindset. The company built a loyal customer base by continually exceeding expectations.

Cultural Transformation: Jobs fostered a culture of innovation and excellence within Apple, promoting continuous learning and development—a clear reflection of the growth mindset (Figure 13.2).

Microsoft's Cultural Transformation with Satya Nadella

Satya Nadella's leadership at Microsoft exemplifies the power of an inclusive mindset and cultural transformation.

Key Elements of Transformation

Cultural Shift: Nadella embraced an inclusive mindset, emphasizing collaboration, diversity, and inclusion. This cultural shift revitalized Microsoft's identity and agility.

Cloud Computing: Microsoft's pivot to cloud computing aligned with an adaptive mindset. Under Nadella's leadership, Azure became a dominant player in the cloud market.

Relevance in Tech Industry: Nadella's adaptive and visionary leadership kept Microsoft relevant in the ever-changing tech industry. The company focused on emerging technologies like AI and IoT.

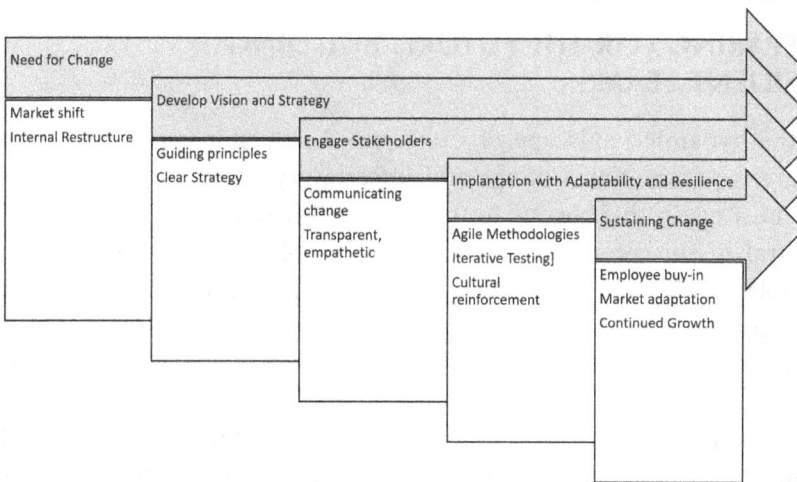

FIGURE 13.2
Case Study Outcomes Flowchart.

SpaceX's Ambitious Goals with Elon Musk

Elon Musk's leadership at SpaceX demonstrates visionary leadership principles in the realm of space exploration.

Key Elements of Ambitious Goals

Vision for the Future: Musk's visionary mindset includes ambitious goals like reducing space exploration costs and making humanity multi-planetary. These objectives inspire and align the team's efforts.

Innovation and Risk-Taking: SpaceX's willingness to innovate and take calculated risks is a testament to the growth mindset. The company has achieved numerous milestones, including reusable rockets.

Resilience in the Face of Challenges: Musk's resilience aligns with the company's pursuit of audacious goals. SpaceX faces numerous technical challenges, but the determination to overcome setbacks is unwavering.

These case studies illustrate how leaders with various mindsets can navigate change and uncertainty successfully. They showcase adaptability, vision, resilience, inclusivity, and innovation as key components of Conscious Leadership in action.

PREPARING FOR THE FUTURE: BUILDING RESILIENT TEAMS

In the dynamic landscape of Conscious Leadership, preparing for the future is paramount. Change and uncertainty are constants, and leaders must equip their teams to thrive in this ever-evolving environment. Central to this preparation is the concept of building resilient teams, capable of withstanding challenges, adapting to change, and emerging stronger.

Resilience, in the context of leadership, refers to a team's ability to bounce back from adversity, setbacks, or disruptions. It involves not only weathering storms but also learning, growing, and thriving through them. Building resilient teams is not a one-time endeavor but an ongoing process rooted in several key principles:

Embrace Change as a Growth Opportunity: Resilient teams understand that change, though often challenging, offers opportunities for growth and development. Leaders instill a growth mindset within their teams, encouraging them to view challenges as chances to learn, adapt, and improve. This mindset shift fosters a culture of continuous learning and innovation.

Cultivate Psychological Safety: A resilient team feels safe to express ideas, share concerns, and take calculated risks. Leaders create an environment where team members can speak up without fear of judgment or reprisal. This psychological safety enables open communication, collaboration, and the exploration of new possibilities.

Promote Adaptability: Resilience is closely tied to adaptability. Leaders help their teams develop the ability to adjust quickly to changing circumstances. This might involve cross-training team members, fostering a culture of experimentation, or encouraging flexible work arrangements.

Foster a Supportive Community: Resilient teams function as a tight-knit community that supports one another. Leaders build camaraderie and trust among team members, encouraging peer support and collaboration. This sense of belonging bolsters individual and collective resilience.

Provide Resources and Training: Resilient teams are well-equipped to face challenges. Leaders invest in resources, training, and development opportunities to ensure that team members have the skills and knowledge needed to overcome obstacles. This proactive approach prepares teams for uncertainty.

Emphasize Well-being: The well-being of team members is a priority for resilient teams. Leaders promote work-life balance, stress management, and mental health support. They recognize that physically and emotionally healthy team members are better prepared to tackle challenges.

Learn from Setbacks: In the face of adversity, resilient teams engage in reflection and learning. Leaders facilitate post-event debriefs to analyze what went well, what could be improved, and how the team can apply these insights to future situations. This practice fosters a culture of continuous improvement.

Set Clear Goals and Objectives: Resilience is fueled by a sense of purpose. Leaders set clear goals and objectives that inspire and motivate their teams. These goals provide a sense of direction and meaning, even in uncertain times.

By focusing on these principles, leaders pave the way for the development of resilient teams that are not only capable of navigating change and uncertainty but also thriving in the midst of them. Resilient teams possess the adaptability, cohesion, and resourcefulness needed to face challenges head-on. They become a source of strength and innovation, driving their organizations forward in an ever-changing world.

As we explore the journey of Conscious Leadership in the subsequent sections, we will delve deeper into the practical strategies and approaches that leaders can employ to build and nurture resilient teams, fostering an environment where both individuals and organizations can thrive.

In the realm of Conscious Leadership, understanding the nature of change and uncertainty is fundamental. Change, an ever-present force in both life and business, carries both opportunities and challenges. Whether driven by external factors like technological advancements and market dynamics or internal shifts such as organizational restructuring and leadership changes, change often brings with it a sense of unpredictability and the potential for unexpected outcomes. This complexity underscores the need for leaders to grasp the essence of change and uncertainty, preparing them to adapt and thrive in a dynamic environment.

When exploring leadership mindsets for navigating ambiguity effectively, it becomes evident that leaders must cultivate specific mental frameworks. These mindsets encompass adaptive, growth, resilient, inclusive, visionary, and Servant Leadership. Each mindset complements the others, forming a comprehensive approach to leadership. The adaptive mindset encourages flexibility, openness to new possibilities, and agility in responding to change. In contrast, the growth mindset views challenges as opportunities for personal and organizational development, emphasizing learning, motivation, and a long-term perspective.

Resilience is a vital component, fostering the ability to bounce back from setbacks and adversity. The inclusive mindset values diverse perspectives and encourages collaboration, while the visionary mindset provides direction and purpose during uncertain times. Lastly, the Servant Leadership mindset prioritizes the well-being of team members, promoting collaboration and empowerment. These leadership mindsets are not mutually exclusive but interconnected, offering a holistic approach to addressing change and uncertainty. Leaders blend these mindsets, selecting the most relevant one for a given context and seamlessly transitioning between them as needed, recognizing that no single mindset is universally applicable.

Tools and strategies for adaptive leadership are essential in the Conscious Leadership journey, aligning with John C. Maxwell's wisdom that leadership is about caring for those under one's charge. Among these tools are scenario planning, agile frameworks, change communication, learning and development programs, resilience training, innovation hubs, crisis management plans, empowerment and delegation, data and analytics, and mentorship and coaching. These tools equip leaders and teams to tackle change and uncertainty effectively, fostering adaptability and resilience.

Real-world case studies provide invaluable insights into the practical application of Conscious Leadership principles in challenging circumstances. Examining cases such as IBM's transformation under Lou Gerstner, Netflix's evolution to streaming, Apple's resurgence with Steve Jobs, Microsoft's cultural transformation led by Satya Nadella, and SpaceX's ambitious goals under Elon Musk showcases how adaptability, vision, resilience, inclusivity, and innovation are key components of successful Conscious Leadership.

In essence, understanding change and uncertainty is pivotal in the Conscious Leadership journey. Leaders must cultivate a variety of interconnected mindsets and utilize a toolbox of strategies and tools to navigate change effectively. These components empower leaders to adapt, inspire resilience, and thrive amidst the ever-evolving landscape of change and uncertainty.

CHAPTER 13 SERVANT LEADERSHIP EXERCISES

These exercises are designed to help you embody Servant Leadership principles, focusing on **serving others, fostering collaboration, and promoting personal growth** within your team. Each activity is structured for individual application and immediate implementation.

Exercise 1: Active Listening Enhancement

Objective: To improve your active listening skills, ensuring team members feel heard and valued.
  Instructions:

- **Identify a Team Member to Engage:**
  - Choose an individual you haven't connected deeply with recently.
  - Schedule a One-on-One Meeting:
  - Allocate at least 30 minutes for an uninterrupted conversation.
  - Practice Active Listening:

- **During the meeting, focus entirely on the speaker.**
  - Avoid interrupting; allow them to express their thoughts fully.
  - Use non-verbal cues (nodding, eye contact) to show engagement. Reflect back what you hear to confirm understanding.
- **Reflect Post-Conversation:**
  - Consider what you learned about the team member.
  - Assess how this deeper understanding can enhance your leadership approach.

Exercise 2: Empowerment through Delegation

Objective: To delegate tasks effectively, fostering team members' growth and autonomy.
  Instructions:

- **Identify a Suitable Task:**
  - Select a task that aligns with a team member's development goals.
  - Choose the Right Team Member.
  - Consider their skills, interests, and current workload.
- **Delegate with Clarity:**
  - Clearly outline the task objectives and expectations. Provide necessary resources and authority.
  - Express confidence in their abilities.
- **Offer Support, Not Micromanagement:**
  - Be available for guidance but allow them autonomy in execution.
- **Review and Provide Feedback:**
  - Upon completion, discuss what went well and areas for improvement. Acknowledge their contributions and growth.

Exercise 3: Servant Leadership Self-assessment

Objective: To evaluate your alignment with Servant Leadership qualities and identify areas for growth.
  Instructions:

- **Reflect on Servant Leadership Traits:**
  - Consider qualities such as empathy, stewardship, commitment to others' growth, and community building.

- **Self-Rate Each Trait:**
  - Use a scale of 1 (needs improvement) to 5 (excellent) to assess yourself on each trait.
- **Identify Areas for Development:**
  - Focus on traits rated 3 or below.
- **Create an Improvement Plan:**
  - For each identified area, outline specific actions to enhance that trait. Set measurable goals and timelines.
- **Seek Feedback:**
  - Discuss your self-assessment with trusted colleagues or mentors to gain additional insights.

Exercise 4: Fostering a Servant Leadership Culture

Objective: To promote a culture of Servant Leadership within your team or organization.

   Instructions:

- **Educate Your Team:**
  - Share the principles of Servant Leadership through workshops or discussions.
- **Model Servant Leadership Behaviors:**
  - Demonstrate humility, empathy, and a focus on serving others in your daily actions.
- **Encourage Peer Recognition:**
  - Implement a system where team members can acknowledge each other's supportive behaviors.
- **Facilitate Community Building:**
  - Organize team activities that strengthen bonds and promote a sense of belonging.
- **Evaluate Progress:**
  - Regularly assess the team's adoption of Servant Leadership principles and celebrate successes.

Exercise 5: Community Service Initiative

Objective: To extend Servant Leadership beyond the workplace by engaging in community service.

Instructions:

- **Identify Community Needs:**
  - Research local organizations or causes that could benefit from support.
- **Organize a Team Volunteer Event:**
  - Plan a volunteer activity that aligns with your team's interests and skills.
- **Participate Actively:**
  - Engage fully in the service activity, demonstrating commitment to the community.
- **Reflect as a Team:**
  - After the event, discuss the experience and its impact on the community and the team.
- **Integrate Learnings:**
  - Consider how the principles practiced during the service can be applied within the workplace.

14

The Intersection of Technology and Conscious Leadership

TECHNOLOGICAL DISRUPTION AND LEADERSHIP RESPONSE

In the modern business landscape, technological disruption is a constant force reshaping industries and challenging established norms. Leaders must adapt and respond effectively to these disruptions to maintain Conscious Leadership practices.

Technological disruption encompasses a wide range of changes driven by innovations in areas such as artificial intelligence, automation, blockchain, and data analytics. These innovations are transforming how businesses operate, interact with customers, and compete in the global market.

Leaders face several critical challenges when dealing with technological disruption:

Adaptability: In the face of rapid technological change, leaders must cultivate adaptability as a core leadership trait. Being open to new ideas and approaches, and encouraging a culture of continuous learning, is essential. Leaders should be willing to embrace change and lead their teams through transitions.

Innovation: To thrive in a disruptive environment, leaders need to foster a culture of innovation within their organizations. This involves encouraging creative thinking, experimentation, and the pursuit of novel solutions to problems. Leaders should also provide the necessary resources and support to drive innovation.

Change Management: Managing change effectively is a vital skill for leaders in times of technological disruption. Leaders must communicate the reasons behind changes, engage with employees, and provide guidance to ensure a smooth transition. Effective change management helps mitigate resistance and ensures buy-in from the team.

DOI: 10.1201/9781003488705-14

Vision and Strategy: Leaders must have a clear vision of how technology can be harnessed to achieve organizational goals. They need to develop strategies that leverage technology to drive growth, enhance efficiency, and deliver value to customers and stakeholders.

Ethical Considerations: As technology advances, leaders must navigate ethical dilemmas related to data privacy, AI ethics, and the impact of technology on society. Leaders should prioritize ethical decision-making, upholding values that align with Conscious Leadership principles.

Learning and Development: To equip their teams with the skills needed to thrive in a tech-disrupted environment, leaders should invest in learning and development programs. These programs ensure that employees have the knowledge and capabilities to leverage technology effectively.

Resilience: In the face of disruptions and challenges, leaders must demonstrate resilience and maintain a positive outlook. Resilient leaders inspire confidence and provide stability during times of uncertainty.

By addressing these challenges, leaders can respond effectively to technological disruption while upholding Conscious Leadership practices. They can guide their organizations through change, foster innovation, and navigate the complex ethical landscape of the tech age.

LEVERAGING TECHNOLOGY FOR CONSCIOUS LEADERSHIP PRACTICES

In the ever-evolving landscape of leadership, technology plays a pivotal role in shaping how leaders interact with their teams, make decisions, and drive organizational success. Conscious leaders recognize the potential of technology as a tool to enhance their leadership practices.

Leaders can leverage technology in various ways to promote Conscious Leadership principles:

Digital platforms and communication tools facilitate seamless interaction among team members, regardless of geographical locations. Leaders can use these tools to foster transparent communication, encourage collaboration, and maintain open channels for feedback and dialogue. Access to data analytics and business intelligence tools empowers leaders to make informed decisions. By harnessing data, leaders can gain valuable insights into team performance, customer preferences, and market trends. This data-driven approach aligns with Conscious Leadership's emphasis on evidence-based decision-making.

Technology enables leaders to embrace virtual teams and remote work arrangements. This flexibility accommodates diverse talent pools, promotes work-life balance, and aligns with Conscious Leadership's focus on inclusivity and employee well-being.

Several digital tools and apps are designed to support mindfulness and well-being. Leaders can encourage their teams to use these resources to manage stress, enhance focus, and maintain mental and emotional health—a fundamental aspect of Conscious Leadership.

Technology allows leaders to share information transparently with their teams. Online dashboards, project management tools, and internal communication platforms promote accessibility to important data and updates, ensuring that everyone is on the same page.

Leaders can invest in e-learning and online training programs to foster continuous learning and development within their teams. This aligns with Conscious Leadership's commitment to personal growth and empowerment.

Automation technologies can streamline repetitive tasks, freeing up time for leaders to focus on more strategic and value-added activities. Leaders can leverage AI and automation to enhance efficiency while ensuring that their teams have the capacity to focus on meaningful work and innovation (Figure 14.1).

ETHICAL CONSIDERATIONS FOR LEADERS IN THE TECH AGE

In an era characterized by rapid technological advancements, leaders are faced with a host of ethical considerations that demand their attention and ethical decision-making. As conscious leaders, they must navigate the complex ethical landscape of the tech age while upholding values that align with their leadership principles.

Some key ethical considerations for leaders in the tech age include data privacy, where the collection and use of personal data have become integral to many tech-driven businesses. Leaders must ensure that their organizations handle data responsibly, respecting individuals' privacy rights, and complying with relevant regulations like GDPR or CCPA.

Another vital ethical consideration is AI ethics, as AI systems, including machine-learning algorithms, are increasingly used for decision-making in various domains. Leaders must consider the ethical implications of AI, such

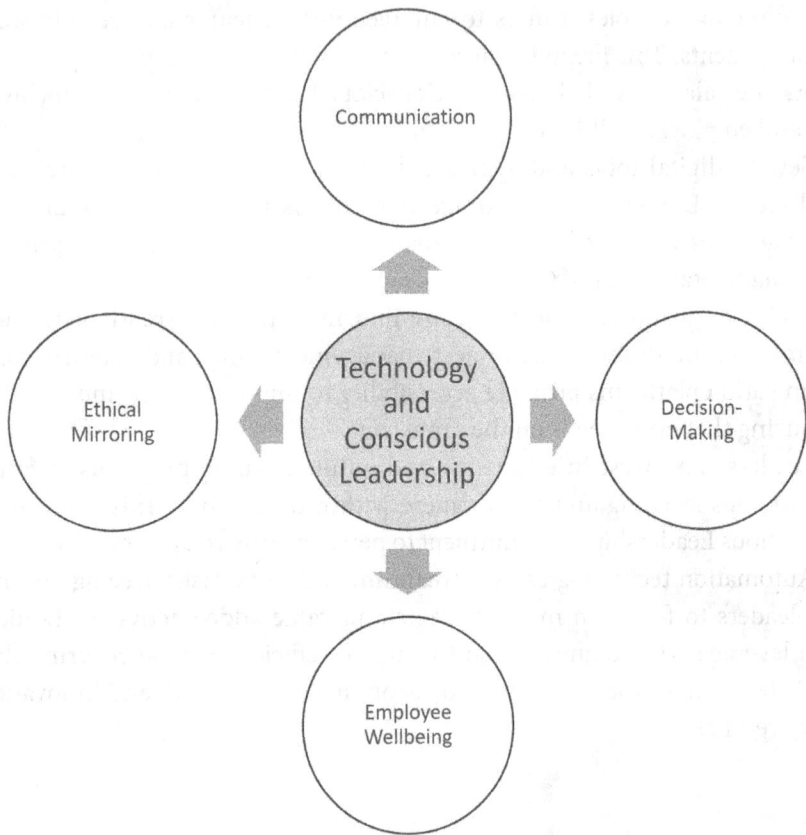

FIGURE 14.1
Technolosgical Tools for Conscious Leaders.

as bias in algorithms, transparency, and accountability. Furthermore, leaders have the opportunity to leverage technology for positive social impact, addressing issues like digital inclusion, sustainability, and social responsibility. Building and maintaining trust with stakeholders, including customers, employees, and investors, is paramount, requiring leaders to be transparent about their technology use, data practices, and business operations.

Cybersecurity is also a significant concern, with the rise of cyber threats and data breaches. Leaders must prioritize cybersecurity measures to protect sensitive information and maintain the trust of their stakeholders.

Regarding employee well-being, leaders must address the potential impact of technology on issues like job security, remote work burnout, and mental health. Proactively supporting their teams' holistic well-being is crucial.

Finally, leaders should consider their organizations' social responsibility, especially in tech companies facing scrutiny over their impact on society. This includes addressing issues related to digital addiction, online misinformation, and the impact of technology on mental health.

Leaders can approach these ethical considerations by integrating ethical frameworks, ethical guidelines, and continuous ethical education within their organizations. They should encourage open discussions about ethical dilemmas and provide channels for employees to raise ethical concerns.

By navigating these ethical challenges with Conscious Leadership principles, leaders can ensure that their organizations contribute positively to society while maintaining their commitment to transparency, integrity, and responsible technology use (Figure 14.2).

CASE STUDIES: CONSCIOUS LEADERSHIP IN TECH COMPANIES

In the ever-evolving landscape of technology and leadership, the intersection of Conscious Leadership principles with the fast-paced, dynamic world of tech companies is a subject of profound importance. To gain deeper insights into this intriguing junction, we turn our attention to case studies that illuminate the embodiment of Conscious Leadership within tech organizations. These real-world examples provide valuable lessons and inspiration for leaders seeking to navigate the challenges and opportunities presented by the tech age.

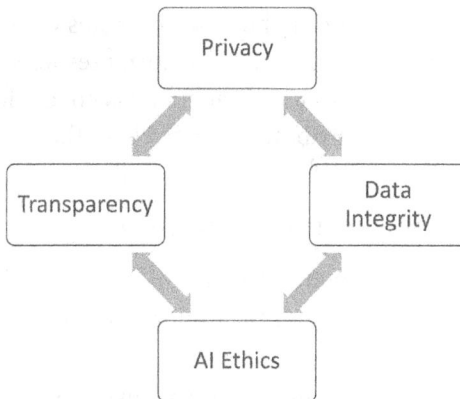

FIGURE 14.2
Ethical Technology Framework.

Google: A Culture of Innovation and Empowerment

Google, the search engine giant, has long been admired not only for its technological prowess but also for its conscious approach to leadership. One striking aspect of Google's leadership philosophy is its commitment to fostering a culture of innovation and empowerment. Leaders at Google encourage employees to dedicate a significant portion of their time to creative projects, a practice known as "20% time." This empowers employees to explore their passions and drive innovation within the company.

Google's leadership understands that Conscious Leadership goes beyond profit margins; it entails nurturing an environment where employees are motivated by purpose and personal growth. The company's commitment to transparency, open communication, and mindfulness programs further exemplifies its Conscious Leadership approach. Google's leaders recognize that fostering a culture of well-being and innovation leads to not only business success but also employee satisfaction and personal growth.

Salesforce: Leading with Social Responsibility

Salesforce, a leader in customer relationship management software, stands out for its Conscious Leadership stance on social responsibility. Under the guidance of CEO Marc Benioff, Salesforce has taken a proactive role in addressing societal issues. Benioff's leadership extends beyond the boardroom as he advocates for equal pay, LGBTQ+ rights, and environmental sustainability.

Salesforce's commitment to Conscious Leadership is reflected in its 1-1-1 philanthropy model, which donates 1% of the company's product, 1% of equity, and 1% of employee time to charitable causes. This model not only makes a positive impact on society but also resonates with employees, aligning their work with a sense of purpose and social responsibility. Salesforce's leadership illustrates that Conscious Leadership is not confined to the corporate world but extends to contributing positively to the broader community.

Microsoft: Embracing Inclusivity and Diversity

Microsoft, under the leadership of Satya Nadella, has undergone a remarkable transformation that highlights the importance of Conscious Leadership in addressing societal challenges.

Nadella's emphasis on inclusivity and diversity has reshaped the company's culture. Microsoft's leaders recognize the value of diverse perspectives and are committed to creating a more inclusive workplace.

One significant step in Microsoft's Conscious Leadership journey is its commitment to accessibility. The company has developed numerous accessibility features in its products, making technology more inclusive for individuals with disabilities. This approach not only aligns with Conscious Leadership principles but also showcases the positive impact tech companies can have on society when they prioritize inclusivity.

Amazon: Balancing Innovation and Responsibility

Amazon, led by Jeff Bezos and later Andy Jassy, represents a tech giant that grapples with the challenges of Conscious Leadership in a rapidly evolving industry. Amazon's leadership has been praised for its relentless innovation, transforming the way we shop and consume media. However, it has also faced criticism related to labor practices, environmental impact, and market dominance.

The case of Amazon underscores the complexities of Conscious Leadership in the tech sector. It prompts leaders to consider how to balance innovation and responsibility, addressing the ethical implications of their actions. Amazon's journey reminds us that Conscious Leadership involves making deliberate choices that align with values and principles, even in the face of immense growth and success.

In conclusion, these case studies of Conscious Leadership in tech companies illustrate the diverse approaches and challenges that leaders face in the ever-evolving tech age. They highlight the importance of fostering innovation, embracing social responsibility, promoting inclusivity, and balancing innovation with ethical considerations. These examples serve as beacons of inspiration for leaders striving to navigate the tech age with purpose, integrity, and a commitment to Conscious Leadership principles. As we reflect on these cases, we find valuable lessons that transcend the tech industry and resonate with leaders in all fields, emphasizing that Conscious Leadership is not merely a choice but a transformative journey toward positive impact and growth.

THE FUTURE OF LEADERSHIP IN AN INCREASINGLY DIGITAL WORLD

As we stand on the threshold of an increasingly digital world, the landscape of leadership is undergoing a profound transformation. The rapid advancement of technology has ushered in an era where digitalization, automation, artificial intelligence, and data analytics are becoming integral to every facet of business and society. In this ever-evolving landscape, the future of leadership is taking on new dimensions, presenting both unprecedented opportunities and unique challenges.

One of the defining characteristics of leadership in an increasingly digital world is adaptability. The pace of technological change is accelerating, and leaders must be agile and open to continuous learning. This adaptability goes hand in hand with a growth mindset, a core principle of Conscious Leadership. Leaders who embrace the idea that challenges are opportunities for growth and learning will thrive in this digital era.

In an environment where data is abundant and easily accessible, data-driven decision-making will be a cornerstone of future leadership. Leaders who can harness the power of data analytics to make informed decisions will have a competitive edge. However, it's not just about collecting data; it's about extracting meaningful insights and translating them into action. The future leader will need to possess strong analytical skills and the ability to see patterns and trends in data.

The concept of "digital leadership" is also emerging as a vital aspect of the future of leadership. Digital leaders are those who can navigate the complexities of the digital landscape, leveraging technology to drive innovation, streamline processes, and enhance customer experiences. They understand the importance of digital transformation and can lead their organizations through it effectively.

Inclusivity and diversity will continue to be key considerations for future leaders. As technology shapes our world, leaders must ensure that the benefits of digitalization are accessible to all, regardless of background or ability. Inclusive leadership involves fostering an environment where diverse voices are heard, and technology is designed with inclusivity in mind.

Ethical leadership will be paramount in an increasingly digital world. With the power and potential for misuse that technology brings, leaders must uphold high ethical standards. They must make decisions that prioritize the well-being of their employees, customers, and society at large. Ethical leadership aligns closely with Conscious Leadership principles, emphasizing values, integrity, and social responsibility.

Another aspect of the future of leadership is the blurring of boundaries between physical and virtual realms. Remote work, virtual teams, and digital collaboration tools are reshaping how work is conducted. Leaders must be adept at managing remote teams, fostering a sense of belonging, and maintaining productivity in a virtual environment.

Furthermore, the rise of artificial intelligence (AI) will redefine the role of leaders. While AI can automate certain tasks, it cannot replace the human qualities of empathy, creativity, and emotional intelligence that are essential in leadership. Leaders of the future will need to strike a balance between leveraging AI for efficiency and preserving the human touch in their leadership approach.

In conclusion, the future of leadership in an increasingly digital world is characterized by adaptability, data-driven decision-making, digital leadership, inclusivity, ethics, virtual collaboration, and the unique blend of human and technological qualities. As we navigate this ever-evolving landscape, Conscious Lmeadership principles provide a guiding light, emphasizing purpose, growth, integrity, and social responsibility. The leaders of tomorrow will be those who embrace these principles and lead with a clear vision, adaptability, and a commitment to positive impact in our digital age.

CHAPTER 14 SELF-AWARENESS EXERCISES

These exercises are designed to deepen your self-awareness, enhance emotional intelligence, and cultivate a leadership style that resonates with authenticity and conscious influence. Each activity is structured for individual application and immediate implementation.

Exercise 1: Self-awareness Journaling

Objective: To enhance self-awareness by reflecting on personal values, beliefs, and behaviors.
   Instructions:

- **Daily Reflection:**
    - Set aside 10–15 minutes each day to journal your thoughts and feelings.
    - Reflect on situations where your actions aligned or conflicted with your core values.
- **Identify Patterns:**
    - After a week, review your entries to identify recurring themes or behaviors.
- **Action Plan:**
    - Develop strategies to reinforce positive behaviors and address areas needing improvement.

Exercise 2: Emotional Intelligence Assessment

Objective: To assess and improve your emotional intelligence (EI) competencies.
   Instructions:

- **Self-assessment:**
  - Complete an EI assessment to evaluate areas such as self-regulation, empathy, and social skills.
- **Feedback from Others:**
  - Seek feedback from colleagues or mentors to gain external perspectives on your EI.
- **Development Plan:**
  - Create a plan to enhance your EI, focusing on identified areas for growth.

Exercise 3: Mindfulness Meditation

Objective: To cultivate mindfulness and present-moment awareness.
   Instructions:

- **Daily Practice:**
  - Dedicate 5–10 minutes each day to mindfulness meditation.
  - Focus on your breath and observe your thoughts without judgment.
- **Application in Leadership:**
  - Apply mindfulness techniques during meetings or decision-making processes to enhance clarity and focus.

Exercise 4: Empathetic Listening

Objective: To improve active listening skills and deepen connections with team members.
   Instructions:

- **One-on-One Conversations:**
  - Engage in regular one-on-one meetings with team members.
- **Listening Techniques:**
  - Practice active listening by giving full attention, avoiding interruptions, and reflecting back what is said.

- **Feedback:**
  - Ask for feedback on your listening skills and make adjustments as needed.

Exercise 5: Vision Articulation

Objective: To clarify and communicate your leadership vision.
  Instructions:

- **Define Your Vision:**
  - Reflect on your long-term goals and the impact you wish to have as a leader.
- **Communicate:**
  - Share your vision with your team, ensuring it aligns with organizational objectives and inspires collective action.
- **Feedback and Adaptation:**
  - Encourage feedback on your vision and be open to refining it based on input.

15

Sustainability and Social Responsibility: The Conscious Leader's Agenda

ANALYZING FAILURES: WHEN CONSCIOUS LEADERSHIP GOES WRONG

In the journey of Conscious Leadership, there are moments when even the most well-intentioned leaders falter. While Conscious Leadership principles guide individuals toward making ethical and responsible decisions, it is essential to recognize that failures can and do occur.

Analyzing these failures provides an opportunity for growth and improvement. By understanding why and how Conscious Leadership can go wrong, leaders can take proactive steps to avoid such pitfalls in the future.

Failures in Conscious Leadership often stem from a misalignment between values and actions. Inauthenticity can lead to a breach of trust among team members and stakeholders. A leader may espouse values such as transparency, integrity, and inclusivity but fail to follow through with actions that reflect these principles. This discrepancy can result in disillusionment and erode the very foundation of Conscious Leadership.

Additionally, leaders may face challenges in balancing competing priorities. The triple bottom line, emphasizing people, planet, and profit, can sometimes lead to dilemmas where difficult decisions must be made. For instance, a leader may grapple with the choice between maximizing profits and investing in sustainable practices that benefit both people and the planet. Failing to find a harmonious balance in such situations can be perceived as a Conscious Leadership failure.

Analyzing these failures requires a deep dive into the root causes. Leaders should reflect on their decisions, actions, and the outcomes they produced. Were there external pressures that influenced the choices made? Did personal biases cloud judgment? Was there a lack of clarity in values or a breakdown

DOI: 10.1201/9781003488705-15

in communication? While the focus of Conscious Leadership is on success and positive impact, understanding where it can falter is equally crucial.

Misalignment with Core Values: One common pitfall is a misalignment between stated values and actions. When leaders fail to uphold the ethical principles they advocate, it erodes trust and credibility. Such inconsistencies can lead to skepticism and disillusionment among employees and stakeholders.

Short-Term Focus: Conscious Leadership often emphasizes long-term sustainability and responsible decision-making. However, leaders may succumb to short-term pressures, compromising on their principles for immediate gains. These shortsighted decisions can harm the organization's reputation and long-term prospects.

Resistance to Change: In some cases, resistance to change can hinder Conscious Leadership efforts. Employees and stakeholders may be reluctant to embrace new practices or principles, even if they align with social responsibility. Leaders must address this resistance through effective communication and education.

Lack of Accountability: A failure to hold individuals or the organization accountable for ethical lapses can undermine Conscious Leadership. Leaders must create a culture of accountability where breaches of ethical standards are addressed promptly and transparently.

Overlooking Stakeholder Needs: Conscious Leadership emphasizes the importance of considering diverse stakeholder needs. When leaders prioritize one group's interests over others or overlook critical stakeholder concerns, it can lead to conflicts and reputational damage.

Inadequate Risk Management: Leaders must navigate risks effectively, especially concerning ethical and social responsibility issues. Failures in risk management can result in ethical scandals or environmental crises that tarnish the organization's image.

Ignoring Employee Well-being: Conscious leaders recognize the significance of employee well-being. Neglecting employees' physical and mental health, work-life balance, or fair compensation can lead to discontent and reduced morale.

Lack of Inclusivity: Fostering inclusivity is a vital aspect of Conscious Leadership. When leaders fail to promote diversity and inclusion within their organizations, they miss out on the benefits of diverse perspectives and may face allegations of discrimination.

Complacency: Some leaders may become complacent once they achieve a certain level of success in Conscious Leadership. This complacency can hinder innovation and prevent leaders from addressing new challenges effectively.

Ineffective Communication: Effective communication is essential in Conscious Leadership, both in conveying values and addressing concerns. Poor communication can lead to misunderstandings, mistrust, and a lack of alignment among stakeholders.

Failure to Adapt: The business and social landscapes are continually evolving. Leaders who fail to adapt their Conscious Leadership strategies to changing circumstances may find their approaches becoming obsolete.

Ignoring External Pressures: External pressures, such as market forces or regulatory changes, can challenge Conscious Leadership efforts. Leaders who ignore these pressures risk falling out of touch with societal expectations and legal requirements.

Lack of Self-awareness: Self-awareness is a cornerstone of Conscious Leadership. Leaders who lack self-awareness may not recognize their own biases, shortcomings, or ethical blind spots, making it difficult to lead responsibly.

Inconsistent Implementation: Consistency is key in Conscious Leadership. Leaders who apply ethical principles selectively or inconsistently may create confusion and undermine their credibility.

Analyzing these failures is not meant to discourage Conscious Leadership but to highlight areas where leaders can falter and how they can learn from these experiences. It's essential for leaders to acknowledge these challenges, reflect on their own leadership practices, and seek continuous improvement.

Leadership is a journey, and setbacks can provide valuable lessons for growth and evolution. By addressing these common pitfalls, conscious leaders can strengthen their commitment to ethical values, social responsibility, and sustainable practices.

Furthermore, leaders should seek feedback and insights from their team members and stakeholders. Open and honest discussions can shed light on areas where Conscious Leadership may have faltered. This introspection and external input are crucial steps in the process of growth and improvement.

Ultimately, analyzing failures in Conscious Leadership is not a condemnation but an opportunity for course correction. It is a reminder that leadership is a continuous journey of learning and adaptation. Through self-awareness, reflection, and a commitment to align values with actions, leaders can navigate the complexities of Conscious Leadership more effectively and with greater success.

Leadership is a journey, and setbacks can provide valuable lessons for growth and evolution. By addressing these common pitfalls, conscious leaders can strengthen their commitment to ethical values, social responsibility, and sustainable practices.

THE TRIPLE BOTTOM LINE: PEOPLE, PLANET, PROFIT

In the realm of Conscious Leadership, the concept of the triple bottom line has gained significant prominence. It encapsulates the idea that businesses and leaders should be accountable for more than just financial profits. Instead, they should consider the impact of their actions on three crucial dimensions: people, planet, and profit.

People: At the heart of Conscious Leadership is a deep concern for the well-being and development of people. This dimension emphasizes the importance of fostering a positive workplace culture, supporting employee growth and empowerment, and nurturing diversity and inclusion. Leaders who prioritize the "people" aspect of the triple bottom line recognize that their teams are not merely resources but individuals with unique talents, aspirations, and needs.

Planet: Conscious leaders understand their role in preserving and protecting the environment. This dimension underscores the significance of sustainable business practices, environmental responsibility, and the reduction of ecological footprints. Leaders committed to the "planet" aspect consider how their decisions impact ecosystems, climate change, and the long-term health of our planet.

Profit: While Conscious Leadership extends beyond financial gain, the "profit" dimension remains a crucial component. Profitability enables organizations to reinvest in their people and the planet. It provides the resources needed to implement sustainable practices, support employee well-being, and contribute positively to society. However, conscious leaders approach profitability with ethics and responsibility, ensuring that it aligns with the broader goals of serving people and safeguarding the planet.

Balancing these three dimensions can be challenging, as they may sometimes seem to conflict with one another. For instance, prioritizing environmental sustainability may initially incur higher costs, impacting short-term profitability. However, conscious leaders recognize that long-term gains in reputation, customer loyalty, and overall sustainability often outweigh immediate financial sacrifices.

Moreover, the triple bottom line aligns closely with the principles of Conscious Leadership. Leaders who embrace this framework tend to exhibit characteristics such as empathy, inclusivity, ethical decision-making, and a long-term perspective. They understand that Conscious Leadership is not a zero-sum game but a holistic approach that benefits all stakeholders.

In conclusion, the triple bottom line provides conscious leaders with a framework for making decisions that consider the well-being of people, the health of the planet, and financial sustainability. It serves as a guiding principle, reminding leaders that their actions have far-reaching consequences. By upholding these values, leaders can create a positive impact that extends beyond their organizations and into the broader world (Figure 15.1).

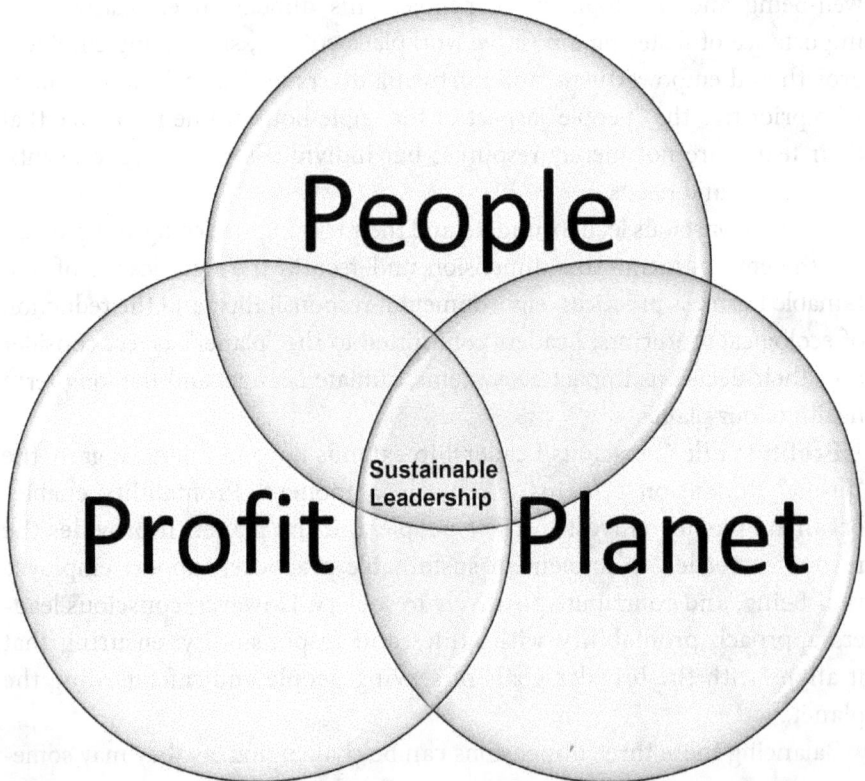

FIGURE 15.1
The Tripple Bottom Line.

IMPLEMENTING SUSTAINABLE PRACTICES IN BUSINESS OPERATIONS

In the pursuit of Conscious Leadership, the integration of sustainable practices into business operations is a crucial step. Leaders who understand the significance of sustainability recognize that it goes beyond compliance with regulations; it becomes an integral part of their organizational culture. Implementing sustainable practices requires a proactive approach that encompasses various aspects of business operations:

Supply Chain Sustainability: Conscious leaders evaluate their supply chains to ensure that the sourcing of materials and products aligns with ethical and sustainable standards. They seek partnerships with suppliers who share their commitment to responsible practices, such as fair labor conditions, reduced environmental impact, and ethical sourcing of raw materials.

Energy Efficiency and Resource Conservation: Sustainability-conscious leaders take steps to minimize energy consumption and reduce resource waste within their operations. They invest in energy-efficient technologies, implement recycling programs, and promote responsible resource management throughout their organizations.

Eco-Friendly Product Development: Leaders committed to sustainability prioritize the development of eco-friendly products and services. They invest in research and innovation to create offerings that have a minimal environmental footprint, whether through reduced emissions, recyclability, or reduced resource consumption.

Community Engagement: Conscious leaders understand their role in contributing positively to the communities in which they operate. They engage with local communities, support social initiatives, and actively seek ways to give back. This engagement fosters goodwill, strengthens relationships, and aligns with the "people" aspect of the triple bottom line.

Employee Engagement: Sustainable practices also extend to employees. Leaders create a workplace culture that promotes sustainability awareness and encourages employees to participate in sustainability initiatives. Engaged employees are more likely to contribute ideas for improvement and actively support sustainability goals.

Transparent Reporting: Transparency is a cornerstone of sustainable business practices. Leaders openly communicate their sustainability efforts, progress, and outcomes to stakeholders, including customers, investors, and the public. Transparent reporting builds trust and accountability.

Continuous Improvement: Sustainable practices are not static; they require continuous improvement. Conscious leaders establish mechanisms for ongoing assessment and refinement of sustainability initiatives. They actively seek feedback from stakeholders to identify areas for enhancement.

Implementing sustainable practices in business operations goes beyond compliance with regulations; it reflects a commitment to ethical leadership and responsible stewardship. Leaders who embrace sustainability understand that their decisions impact not only their organizations but also society and the environment at large.

Moreover, sustainability aligns with the principles of Conscious Leadership. It requires empathy, a long-term perspective, ethical decision-making, and a genuine concern for the well-being of people and the planet. Sustainable leaders recognize that their success is intertwined with the well-being of all stakeholders, and they actively work to create a positive and lasting impact.

In summary, conscious leaders integrate sustainable practices into various facets of their business operations, promoting responsible stewardship of resources, ethical decision-making, and a commitment to the well-being of people and the planet. Sustainability is not just a business strategy; it is a reflection of an organization's values and a testament to Conscious Leadership.

SOCIAL RESPONSIBILITY AS A LEADERSHIP MANDATE

Conscious leadership extends beyond the confines of organizational boundaries and encompasses a broader perspective on societal well-being. Social responsibility is a vital element of Conscious Leadership, emphasizing a leader's duty to contribute positively to society. Leaders who embrace social responsibility recognize that their actions can have a profound impact on communities, stakeholders, and the world at large.

Community Engagement: Socially responsible leaders actively engage with and support the communities in which their organizations operate. They identify community needs, initiate partnerships with local organizations, and invest in initiatives that address pressing social issues. This engagement fosters a sense of shared responsibility and goodwill.

Diversity, Equity, and Inclusion: Conscious leaders champion diversity, equity, and inclusion within their organizations. They create inclusive workplaces that value diverse perspectives, experiences, and backgrounds.

By promoting equal opportunities and fair treatment, they contribute to broader societal goals of social justice and equality.

Philanthropy and Giving Back: Socially responsible leaders recognize their capacity to make a positive impact through philanthropic efforts. They allocate resources and financial support to charitable causes aligned with their values. Whether through donations, grants, or volunteering, they actively give back to society.

Environmental Stewardship: Sustainability and environmental consciousness are integral aspects of social responsibility. Leaders who prioritize environmental stewardship reduce their organizations' environmental footprint, promote eco-friendly practices, and actively support conservation efforts. By doing so, they contribute to the well-being of the planet and future generations.

Ethical Business Practices: Ethical behavior in business is a cornerstone of social responsibility. Leaders uphold high ethical standards in their dealings with customers, partners, employees, and stakeholders. They prioritize honesty, integrity, and transparency, setting an example for ethical conduct in the broader business community.

Humanitarian Initiatives: Socially responsible leaders often engage in humanitarian initiatives that address critical global challenges. These initiatives may focus on issues such as poverty alleviation, healthcare access, education, and disaster relief. Through their leadership, they inspire collective action to tackle pressing societal issues.

Advocacy and Thought Leadership: Leaders who champion social responsibility often become advocates for causes they are passionate about. They use their influence and platforms to raise awareness, advocate for policy changes, and drive social progress. Their thought leadership extends beyond their organizations, inspiring others to join in creating a better world.

Global Impact: Socially responsible leaders understand the interconnectedness of the global community. They consider the impact of their decisions on a global scale and seek to address international challenges, such as human rights violations, global health crises, and climate change. Their leadership transcends borders and contributes to global solutions.

Measuring Impact: Measuring the impact of social responsibility initiatives is essential for conscious leaders. They establish clear metrics and key performance indicators (KPIs) to assess the effectiveness of their efforts. Regular reporting and evaluation ensure that resources are directed toward initiatives that create meaningful change.

Inspiring Others: Perhaps one of the most significant aspects of social responsibility as a leadership mandate is the power to inspire others. Leaders who lead by example, demonstrating their commitment to social responsibility, inspire employees, peers, and stakeholders to embrace similar principles. This ripple effect magnifies the positive impact on society.

In summary, social responsibility is a defining element of Conscious Leadership, reflecting a leader's commitment to contributing positively to society. It encompasses community engagement, diversity and inclusion, philanthropy, ethical practices, humanitarian initiatives, advocacy, global impact, and the inspiration of others. Socially responsible leaders recognize their role in shaping a better world and actively work toward that vision.

MEASURING SOCIAL AND PROFESSIONAL RESPONSIBILITY

In the realm of Conscious Leadership, measuring social and professional responsibility is not only about quantifying impact but also about ensuring accountability and continuous improvement.

Leaders who are truly committed to their roles as responsible stewards of their organizations and society understand the importance of metrics and assessment tools. By measuring the extent of their social and professional responsibility, they gain insights into areas that require attention and can refine their strategies for a more meaningful impact.

Key Performance Indicators (KPIs): Conscious leaders establish KPIs to track their organization's performance in areas related to social and professional responsibility. These indicators are specific, measurable, and aligned with their objectives. For instance, they may measure employee diversity, energy efficiency, or the percentage of profits allocated to charitable giving. KPIs provide a clear picture of progress.

Transparency and Reporting: Transparency is a fundamental aspect of responsible leadership. Leaders are transparent about their organization's practices, policies, and performance related to social responsibility. They produce regular reports that communicate their efforts and achievements to stakeholders, fostering trust and accountability.

Sustainability Reporting: Sustainability reports have become a standard practice for organizations committed to social and environmental responsibility. These reports detail an organization's sustainability initiatives, environmental impact, and social contributions. Leaders ensure that these reports adhere to recognized standards and are independently verified.

Impact Assessments: Leaders engage in impact assessments to evaluate the effects of their social and professional responsibility initiatives. This involves conducting comprehensive analyses of the outcomes and consequences of their actions. Impact assessments can identify areas where improvements are needed and guide future decision-making.

Ethical Audits: Ethical audits are systematic reviews of an organization's ethical practices and adherence to established ethical guidelines. Leaders may employ internal or external auditors to assess their organization's ethical conduct, identifying areas of non-compliance or potential risks.

Stakeholder Feedback: Leaders actively seek feedback from stakeholders, including employees, customers, partners, and the communities they serve. Stakeholder input provides valuable insights into how their actions are perceived and how they can better meet the needs and expectations of those they impact.

Benchmarking: Benchmarking involves comparing an organization's social and professional responsibility practices to industry peers or recognized standards. Leaders use benchmarking to identify best practices and areas where they can excel or improve. It provides a competitive context for their efforts.

Continuous Improvement: Conscious leaders embrace a culture of continuous improvement in social and professional responsibility. They understand that the journey toward responsible leadership is ongoing and evolving. Feedback, data, and insights are used to refine strategies and initiatives.

Alignment with Sustainable Development Goals (SDGs): Many leaders align their social responsibility efforts with the United Nations' Sustainable Development Goals (SDGs). These global goals provide a framework for addressing pressing societal and environmental challenges. Leaders identify which SDGs are most relevant to their organization's mission and incorporate them into their strategies.

Ethical Decision-Making Frameworks: Leaders implement ethical decision-making frameworks within their organizations. These frameworks provide guidelines for assessing the ethical implications of decisions and actions. They help leaders navigate complex ethical dilemmas and ensure that their choices align with responsible leadership principles.

Public Recognition and Awards: Leaders who excel in social and professional responsibility often receive public recognition and awards. These accolades acknowledge their commitment and inspire others to follow suit. However, conscious leaders remain humble and view these accolades as opportunities to further their mission rather than as the end goal.

In conclusion, measuring social and professional responsibility is an integral aspect of Conscious Leadership. Leaders employ various tools and approaches, including KPIs, transparency, sustainability reporting, impact assessments, ethical audits, stakeholder feedback, benchmarking, and alignment with SDGs. These measures ensure accountability, foster continuous improvement, and demonstrate a commitment to creating a positive impact on society and the profession.

CHAPTER 15 AUTHENTICITY AND ETHICS EXERCISES

These exercises are designed to deepen your self-awareness, enhance emotional intelligence, and foster a leadership style rooted in authenticity and conscious influence. Each activity is structured for individual application and immediate implementation.

Exercise 1: Values Clarification

Objective: To identify and align your personal values with your leadership practices.

   Instructions:

- **Identify Core Values:**
  - List your top five personal values (e.g., integrity, empathy, innovation).
- **Reflect on Alignment:**
  - Evaluate how your daily leadership actions reflect these values.
- **Action Plan:**
  - Develop strategies to better align your behaviors with your core values.

Exercise 2: Mindful Decision-Making

Objective: To incorporate mindfulness into your decision-making process.

Instructions:

- **Pause and Reflect:**
  - Before making a significant decision, take a moment to breathe deeply and center yourself.
- **Assess Implications:**
  - Consider the potential impact of your decision on all stakeholders involved.
- **Make Conscious Choices:**
  - Choose actions that align with your values and promote the greater good.

Exercise 3: Emotional Regulation

Objective: To enhance your ability to manage emotions effectively.
Instructions:

- **Self-Monitoring:**
  - Observe and note situations that trigger strong emotional responses.
- **Develop Coping Strategies:**
  - Implement techniques such as deep breathing, mindfulness, or reframing to manage your reactions.
- **Reflect and Adjust:**
  - Regularly assess the effectiveness of your strategies and make necessary adjustments.

Exercise 4: Active Listening

Objective: To improve communication and strengthen relationships through active listening.
Instructions:

- **Engage Fully:**
  - During conversations, give your full attention without interrupting.
- **Reflect and Clarify:**
  - Summarize what the other person has said to ensure understanding.
- **Respond Thoughtfully:**
  - Provide feedback that acknowledges their perspective and contributes constructively.

Exercise 5: Continuous Learning

Objective: To commit to ongoing personal and professional development.
 Instructions:

- **Identify Growth Areas:**
  - Determine skills or knowledge you wish to enhance.
- **Set Learning Goals:**
  - Establish specific, measurable objectives for your development.
- **Pursue Development Opportunities:**
  - Engage in relevant courses, workshops, or mentorship programs.

Bibliography

Bechara, A., & Damasio, A. R. (2005). The somatic marker hypothesis: A neural theory of economic decision. *Games and Economic Behavior*, 52(2), 336–372.

Brown, B. (2012). *Daring Greatly: How the Courage to Be Vulnerable Transforms the Way We Live, Love, Parent, and Lead*. Gotham Books.

Caligiuri, P. (2012). *Cultural Agility: Building a Pipeline of Successful Global Professionals*. Jossey-Bass.

Cross, R., Rebele, R., & Grant, A. (2016). Collaborative overload. *Harvard Business Review*, January–February.

Damasio, A. R. (1994). *Descartes' Error: Emotion, Reason, and the Human Brain*. Putnam Publishing.

Dweck, C. S. (2006). *Mindset: The New Psychology of Success*. Random House.

Edmondson, A. C. (1999). Psychological safety and learning behavior in work teams. *Administrative Science Quarterly*, 44(2), 350–383.

Eurich, T. (2017). *Insight: Why We're Not as Self-Aware as We Think, and How Seeing Ourselves Clearly Helps Us Succeed at Work and in Life*. Crown Business.

Goleman, D. (1995). *Emotional Intelligence: Why It Can Matter More Than IQ*. Bantam Books.

Goleman, D. (1998). What makes a leader? *Harvard Business Review*, November–December.

Greenleaf, R. K. (1977). *Servant Leadership: A Journey into the Nature of Legitimate Power and Greatness*. Paulist Press.

Kahneman, D. (2011). *Thinking, Fast and Slow*. Farrar, Straus and Giroux.

Kaiser, R. B., & Hogan, R. (2011). How to (and how not to) assess the integrity of managers. *Consulting Psychology Journal: Practice and Research*, 63(4), 227–242.

Klein, G. (1999). *Sources of Power: How People Make Decisions*. MIT Press.

Marcario, R. (2021). Leading with purpose. *Harvard Business Review Digital Articles*.

Maslow, A. H. (1943). A theory of human motivation. *Psychological Review*, 50(4), 370–396.

Mbigi, L., & Maree, J. (1995). *Ubuntu: The Spirit of African Transformation Management*. Knowledge Resources.

Myers, D. G. (2002). *Intuition: Its Powers and Perils*. Yale University Press.

Ragins, B. R., & Kram, K. E. (Eds.). (2007). *The Handbook of Mentoring at Work: Theory, Research, and Practice*. SAGE Publications.

Schön, D. A. (1983). *The Reflective Practitioner: How Professionals Think in Action*. Basic Books.

Siegel, D. J. (2007). *The Mindful Brain: Reflection and Attunement in the Cultivation of Well-Being*. W. W. Norton & Company.

Sinek, S. (2009). *Start with Why: How Great Leaders Inspire Everyone to Take Action*. Portfolio.

World Bank. (2020). *World Development Report 2020: Trading for Development in the Age of Global Value Chains*. World Bank Publications.

World Economic Forum. (2020). *Global Social Mobility Report 2020: Equality, Opportunity and a New Economic Imperative*.

Zenger, J., & Folkman, J. (2019). The skills leaders need at every level. *Harvard Business Review Digital Articles*.

Index

For Product Safety Concerns and Information please contact our EU
representative GPSR@taylorandfrancis.com
Taylor & Francis Verlag GmbH, Kaufingerstraße 24, 80331 München, Germany

www.ingramcontent.com/pod-product-compliance
Lightning Source LLC
Chambersburg PA
CBHW061308220326
41599CB00026B/4788

*9 7 8 1 0 3 2 7 8 6 1 3 1 *